• HALSGROVE DISCOVER SERIES ➤

# UNUSUAL PUBS
## AMAZING STORIES

120 remarkable licensed premises
to visit around Britain

## BOB BARTON

HALSGROVE

First published in Great Britain in 2020
Copyright © Bob Barton 2020

Title page photograph: *The White Horse, Hedgerley.*
*Pictured are the Datchet Border Morris Men, shortly before*
*their January 'wassail' in the adjacent orchard.*

British Library Cataloguing-in-Publication Data
A CIP record for this title is available from the British Library

ISBN 978 0 85704 347 4

**HALSGROVE**
Halsgrove House,
Ryelands Business Park,
Bagley Road, Wellington, Somerset TA21 9PZ
Tel: 01823 653777   Fax: 01823 216796
email: sales@halsgrove.com

Part of the Halsgrove group of companies
Information on all Halsgrove titles is available at:
www.halsgrove.com

Printed and bound in India by Parksons Graphics Ltd

*Opposite: A thirst-inducing line-up of ales on the bar of*
*the Three Tuns Inn, Bishop's Castle (page 27).*

# CONTENTS

# ACKNOWLEDGEMENTS

VISITING PUBS has always been a favourite occupation of mine, and it has been particularly enjoyable when in the company of my partner Sue Adie. Our explorations 'off the beaten track' in Worcestershire and Shropshire beat any overseas holiday hands-down. Sue's reading of my original text and her painstaking proof-reading are also greatly appreciated. Pub visits with friends James Young, John Weale and Nick Markson (notably in Greater Manchester after our annual visit to the city's beer festival at Manchester Central) have also been fun. Similarly with Richard Tippett, with whom I fulfilled an ambition to visit London's famous 'rock-café', the Troubadour and, somewhat more energetically, trekked across Kent's Isle of Grain. This was in the footsteps of artist William Hogarth, to visit his eponymous inn (suggested by James Young). My daughter Joanna 'discovered' the Rye Waterworks micropub.

I must thank historian Geoff Wellens for giving me an impromptu tour of the Olde Boar's Head, Middleton; and Neil Wooler for introducing me to the delightful Little R'ale House on Wellingborough station, during one of our railway pub-themed get-togethers. Ray and Lindsey Peacock suggested Ye Cracke, Liverpool. Thank you also to readers of my previous books, *Unusual Railway Pubs, Refreshment Rooms and Ale Trains*, and *Unusual Pubs by Boot, Bike and Boat*, whose interest has energized me to produce this third volume. I raise my glass to the editors of the Campaign for Real Ale's (CAMRA) regional magazines and members of its Pub Heritage Group, whose work provides me with constant inspiration. I must not forget the licensees and staff of the pubs featured herein, deserving of special mention for their patience and dedication. They go 'the extra mile' making their establishments welcoming to demanding and inquisitive customers such as myself.

*Bob Barton, Hayes, Middlesex*

## PHOTOGRAPHIC CREDITS

All photographs are by the author, or from his collection, except the following, courtesy of:

The Harry Kelly Collection, Queensferry History Group, page 6. Walsall Museum Service, page 11. Creative Commons, 'Lamberhurst', page 12. M.J. Cheetham, page 13 (top). Creative Commons, Immanuel Giel, page 20 (top). Creative Commons, Manfred Heyde, page 33 (bottom). Creative Commons, 'Verbcatcher', page 35. Creative Commons, Edgar El, page 45. Wikimedia Commons, pages 67 (top), 74. The Bishopsgate Institute, page 83. Creative Commons, Tim Green, page 95. Flickr Creative Commons, John Harvey Pegg, page 127.

Every effort has been made to contact copyright holders and we apologize for any unintentional omissions which will be rectified in future editions.

# INTRODUCTION

EVERYONE LOVES A GOOD STORY. That's one of the reasons we visit attractions such as museums, historic houses and castles. It is why we eagerly take our seats at the cinema or theatre. Why not visit the pub for a story too? This is a pub guide with a difference. Instead of focusing on ale, food or décor, I have selected licensed premises on the basis of their role in a tale or two. Expect to read stories of bravery, crime, heroism and escape, for example. Some heart-warming, others heart-rending. Tales historical, legendary or thought-provoking. There is also a spattering of eccentric people, quirky events and customs, often with their roots firmly in folklore. At risk of stating the obvious, an added bonus is that, if you venture to visit these places, you'll sample some fine ale and food along the way. (Though please note that, even in the 2020s, not all pubs serve meals.)

We are lucky to have houses in towns, villages and cities, throughout Britain, that anyone can enter without needing an invitation. On doing so they (in most cases) feel immediately at their ease. These *public* houses have been part of our way of life for centuries. They continue to be a source of relaxation and enjoyment at a time when the world seems an increasingly stressful place. Throughout my adult life, I've 'popped into the pub' wherever I've travelled and, though I've enjoyed the refreshment and company, I've often found information about their past lacking. History and mythology surrounding pubs and inns is a sorely neglected field – certainly compared to other examples of the built environment, such as churches, stately homes and monuments.

The response by readers to my first book, *Unusual Railway Pubs, Refreshment Rooms and Ale Trains* (Halsgrove, 2013/2018), was positive. At first, I thought this was because the subjects of railways and real ale are symbiotic. But there is something deeper: I discovered it tapped into a common love, not just of trains, but of nostalgia and journeys generally. In my second book, *Unusual Pubs by Boot, Bike and Boat* (Halsgrove, 2017), I included establishments that were not only quirky but could also be visited as part of days out and longer leisure trips. One of the establishments I discovered was the Locks Inn – an entrancing hostelry at Geldeston, isolated amid the reed-fringed marshes of Norfolk. It hosts regular story nights, when storytelling sessions (with titles such as 'Midwinter Magic – Tales and Ales') take place in the candle-lit bar, usually accompanied by lashings of mulled cider. It set me thinking, why not find stories that – if they could talk – pubs themselves would tell? From that germ of an idea comes this third selection of pubs. This time, those deemed unusual, not for their wonky structure nor collection of strange hats, but for something customers can't normally see.

My research has been the perfect excuse to travel around this wonderful country and drink real ale in some remarkable establishments. Whether you are an armchair pubgoer or an active one, I hope you enjoy the journey as much as I. *Hitchcock's local, page 83.*

# 1. 'DIANE WELCOMES YOU TO THE MADHOUSE'
## Why the best stories begin at the pub

EARLY IN ROBERT LOUIS STEVENSON'S NOVEL *Kidnapped*, his hero David Balfour describes the first sighting of the inn where his troubles would begin:

> At the end of the pier…and backed against a pretty garden of holly-trees and hawthorns, I could see the building which they called the Hawes Inn.

Delivered by his miserly uncle Ebenezer, there they meet a tall ship's captain. Seated by a fire, he is dressed in a thick jacket and a 'tall hairy cap drawn down over his ears.' Soon lured aboard the sea-dog's sailing ship, David – who has never even visited the coast before – is trapped on board and bound for North America, to be sold into slavery in the Carolinas…

The Hawes Inn still stands, in South Queensferry near Edinburgh, alongside the towering ramparts of the Forth Bridge. It is unlikely Stevenson would have seen the completed bridge, and the inn has grown a little in size since he stayed, but it continues to offer accommodation and retains a garden of holly-trees and hawthorns. On my arrival, there was no landlord smoking a pipe at the door. Inside, however, I was pleased to see a flagstone floor, a blazing fire and, like the book's protagonists, enjoyed a thirst-quenching ale. (The malty and warming Lia Fail from Inveralmond Brewery.) Like Charles Dickens, Stevenson – at least before he left British shores on his travels – was an inveterate pub-goer. Both authors found inns an abundant source of inspiration.

In Dickens' last novel, *Our Mutual Friend*, readers are introduced to a prim landlady with the manner of a schoolmistress. Miss Abbey Potterson keeps her inn, the Six Jolly Fellowship Porters,

*A busy scene outside the Hawes Inn, South Queensferry, in the Edwardian era. It was used to great effect by Robert Louis Stevenson in his novel* Kidnapped.

'respectable.' The author describes the hostelry at length, down to the red curtains 'matching the noses of the regular customers' and

> Exactly at the closing hour, all the guests who were left, filed out in the best order: Miss Abbey standing at the half-door of the bar, to hold a ceremony of review and dismissal. All wished Miss Abbey good-night and Miss Abbey wished good-night to all…

Many will recognise the pub as the Grapes in London's Limehouse (page 85) – which Dickens certainly visited. Hard by the river, it retains its bare-boards atmosphere and modest dimensions. You can still squeeze into an area 'not much larger than a hackney-coach' to quaff beer served 'from polite beer-pulls that made low bows when customers were served.'

Many other writers, such as Jerome K. Jerome (in *Three Men in a Boat*) and Hilaire Belloc, adored pubs and featured them in their novels. Belloc, known for the oft-quoted 'When you have lost your inns, drown your empty selves, for you will have lost the last of England,' devised a wonderful pub crawl that can still be followed. It traverses a hundred miles of Sussex countryside, described in his delightful *The Four Men – a Farrago*. Each of the four characters in the book – the Sailor, the Poet, Grizzlebeard and 'Myself'– represent a different aspect of his personality as it changes through his life (page 22). Laurie Lee, whose autobiographical *Cider With Rosie* recalls his growing up in a Gloucestershire valley is, on the other hand, associated with one pub, his beloved local, the Woolpack (page 114). Nothing moved faster than a horse, he remembered. The 'first brass-lamped motor car steaming up the valley' heralded the end of an era; the finalé of a lifestyle directed by the local squire.

The stone-built Woolpack, with its bare wood floors, outside loos and ageing piano, rises like a rocky outcrop from the valley floor. When I called recently, men were sitting outside on benches discussing the latest football scores – probably just as they did in Laurie's time – while a family played cards on the vine-fringed terrace. Another gaggle of locals was ensconced in an inner sanctum closest to the all-important bar, whose pump-clips promised foaming pints of Uley Bitter. Though I never met the author, a signed copy of *Cider With Rosie*, given to me by a friend in this pub many years before the writer's death in 1997, is one of my most treasured possessions.

Pubs and bars are frequently the settings for jokes. How many, I wonder, start with that classic line 'A horse walks into a bar...'? While researching this book, I visited a pub in rural Hertfordshire – the Plough at King's Walden – where that is said to have actually happened. An old boy called Ted Dobson, a farrier, was a regular and quite a character (he once got into a fight in the bar over a game of dominoes). Said the landlord of the time: 'Another of Ted's wrong moves was when he turned left instead of right when he took a horse into the pub. It got well stuck and it took him ages

to get it back out!' (p157, *Tales From the Country Pub*, Martin, B.P.). The current licensee confirmed the story is true: 'It was a deliberate act – he simply didn't want to leave his horse unattended outside, he said.' One can imagine the creature ill-at-ease in the small, crowded bar, with customers laughing loudly and nursing their drinks to avoid them being knocked over by the unwieldy animal.

Like many a country pub, the Plough was once full of individuals such as Ted. In a corner is a chair bearing a brass memorial to another, one Artie Hale. A regular from 1938 until his death in his nineties, he had visited regularly after being demobbed (he became a paratrooper in World War Two). Artie was often worse for drink and, on such occasions, took to sleeping in a campervan in the car park, cooking himself breakfast on a primus stove. He once reminisced: 'The local police superintendent sometimes acted as my alarm clock...he'd bang on the van window to make sure I got up in time for work.'

*The sign at the Woolpack in Slad, recalls writer Laurie Lee's youth 'when nothing moved faster than a horse.'*

*The Plough, King's Walden, where locals tell the story of a horse entering the bar.*

There is a wassailing tradition in South Wales where a horse (a man imitating a horse, to be precise) is taken into pubs and houses. This takes place in early January and is called Mari Lwyd, meaning grey mare or grey Mary. There are two accompanying groups, one of which sings outside the pub with the 'horse', asking to enter. The other group, standing inside, responds in song that he cannot. A musical duel in Welsh ensues, to-and-fro until the gang indoors relents. Then everyone piles in for liquid refreshment. I witnessed an example in 2020, at the Harrison pub off the Gray's Inn Road. A group from the London Welsh Centre did it as a pub crawl. The atmosphere was jovial and the pub rammed, though the singing wasn't quite up to male-voice choir standards.

We all have our favourite pubs and among the main reasons (apart from their beer or food) is because we enjoy their atmosphere. We are comfortable with their location and 'feel'. Often subconsciously, we select those where fellow customers are most like us; where our stories, and those of our friends, have been enacted and played out. A pub is like a theatre; a public stage for get-togethers of many kinds. Our fellow actors may be friends, family, colleagues, associates, lovers, club members, musicians or dancers. Whoever they are – to continue the analogy – they're participants in our own comedy, farce, drama, intrigue or romance. Laura Thompson, in her joyous book about her grandmother's pub, *The Last Landlady*, takes the theatrical link further:

In those days there were licensing hours, which placed a limit upon pleasure in a very English way. The twice-daily closing and opening…exactly like theatre: lights up and down, make-up on and off, matinée and evening. Also theatrical was the separation between the bars, 'out front' and the living quarters: backstage.

Sometimes, we remember the stories shared by everyone in the pub at the time (such as the horse-in-bar event described above) or, more often, they only relate to our particular circle. The time Jim slipped over and caused other people to spill their beer while miraculously keeping his pint upright. Or the case of mistaken identity which caused extreme embarrassment and hilarious laughter in equal measure…

Pub 'do you remember' stories can be intensely personal. I vividly recall a pub in South London's Stamford Street, the

*A man dressed as a ghostly horse is led to the door of the Harrison, off London's Gray's Inn Road, during the Mari Lwyd celebration, in 2020. Singers inside and outside the pub partake in a musical 'duel' (in Welsh) before the equine figure is allowed to enter.*

Brunswick Arms (now demolished) where, as a shy eighteen-year-old I nervously asked the young barmaid out on a date. Just as I remember the one up the road where, a few days later, she stood me up (they were playing an album by The Carpenters as I waited in vain – *Rainy Days and Mondays, et al* – making that evening even more depressing for me). When I eventually succeeded in getting a date with her (after she'd taken me home to be vetted by her mother) we visited a pub which closed shortly afterwards. The Pig and Whistle near Southall is now a McDonald's restaurant. It's hardly surprising our relationship didn't get off the ground. Then there are the pubs used when courting, or having a reunion with a long-lost friend or stopping off *en route* to honeymoon; I could go on, we all have our own examples.

I once worked in an office overlooking a Hammersmith pub, the Builders Arms, with a bird's-eye view of its comings and goings. It was, and still is, a Young's house (since renamed the Hammersmith Ram). A weekly visitor was the lumbering brewer's dray, bringing the beer and pulled by a pair of large horses. Somehow, they navigated their way through London's traffic from the brewery in Wandsworth, with two bowler-hatted draymen in charge. That pub was the nearest we had to a staff canteen and many a colleague's birthday, promotion or departure was celebrated. Not to mention lunch hours and evenings spent gossiping, flirting or dissing our bosses, in equal measure. I recall one particularly lively Christmas Eve afternoon when the place was packed to the gunnels, carol sheets were passed round and slurred carol singing was attempted. Such scenes in pubs are now consigned to the past (certainly in London). Those personal memories are precious and I hope you have many of your own.

Though I'm not a fan of background music in pubs, there are notable exceptions. Who hasn't had a favourite pub jukebox? Mine was in the Blue Posts, a Charrington's tied house, now demolished, in Tottenham Court Road and visited in the early 1970s. Clichéd motorbiking ballads, such as *Leader of the Pack* from the Shangri-las and *Terry* by Twinkle, blasted out from this brightly-lit Wurlitzer, into a smoke-filled bar crowded with after-work drinkers. We all have tracks that, every time we hear them, remind us which pub we were in, when and with whom (for me, one is Lou Reed's *Walk on the Wild Side*). Also memorable are the pubs visited on the day of a momentous event – such as the death of Elvis Presley or shooting of John Lennon. On days like those, there is only one topic of bar-room conversation.

Inns and storytelling have gone together since time immemorial. In medieval times, strolling players and bands of actors plied their trade in and around them. Though fiction, Chaucer's *Canterbury Tales*, with pilgrims as his mouthpieces, as they trudged from tavern to inn, was surely inspired by real life. The young Bard himself, William Shakespeare, was not above partaking in a pub crawl (page 26) and what entertaining occasions they must have been. These days, storytelling events at pubs – hosted by charismatic narrators and often illuminated by candle-light for added

*Lewis Tumbleweed Parker, at work in the Bottle of Sauce, Cheltenham, where he was resident poet.*

*The Moon Inn, Mordiford, where the author heard a folk tale about a local dragon.*

*St George slays the Dragon, as he does each Boxing Day, in a play put on by the St Albans Mummers. The pub in the background is the town's Ye Olde Fighting Cocks, one of the oldest in England.*

effect – continue the tradition. They are not yet widely staged but I heartily recommend going along if you find one. I stumbled upon an interesting variation when I met Lewis Tumbleweed Parker in a busy Cheltenham pub, the Bottle of Sauce. Wearing a trilby, he was seated at a table in the snug, behind a portable typewriter. A notice informed customers: 'Poet for hire'. Part of the town's annual Festival of Literature, he was employed to tap out lines on whatever theme was requested by customers. They were thoughtful lines, too, which I found surprising, especially as he was drinking nothing more inspirational than water.

Storytelling has a natural home in the pub. Many landlords were adept at weaving a good yarn, as exemplified by Will Ritson (1808-90). This Victorian publican's outrageous tall stories attracted customers to his pub in the Cumbrian fells, on dark and otherwise quiet autumn nights. His skills as a raconteur are still celebrated annually at the World's Biggest Liar Competition (page 112) which attracted an audience of about one hundred when I attended. Sometimes, though, it's a fellow customer, rather than a performer

on a stage, who turns out to be a master storyteller. I was in a half-timbered pub in a Herefordshire village (the Moon Inn at Mordiford, drinking a moreish Otter Brewery Amber) when I got talking to a chap clutching a walking stick and nursing a pint. He told a spell-binding tale about a terrifying wild creature called the Mordiford Dragon, that used to descend from the woods to drink in the River Lugg. When it began killing and devouring the locals, it was hunted down by a brave fellow who attacked it with a lance, he said. He described the events as though they had occurred yesterday, or last week, before adding "There was a painting of it in the church until the 1800s, when the vicar got rid of it."

Plays about England's patron saint, St George, slaying a dragon have been performed outside pubs since at least the fifteenth century. Performed by Mummers, they are as much part of the Christmas season as plum pudding and tinsel. They also star a Turkish knight, Beelzebub, a Doctor and Father Christmas and always have a happy ending. Ancient stories about a huge Black Dog, or 'Black Shuck' – invariably with bright red eyes the size of saucers – are more sinister but still do the rounds at storytelling nights. These days, the fearsome creature looms ahead of the viewer on a lonely drive home at night (it never seems to happen in daylight, or when the car has passengers). 'Only a fool would take that road late at night,' a bright spark at the bar will remark, while shaking his head. Carolyne Larrington, author of *The Land of the Green Man* says that one pub sign, at the Black Dog on Jersey's Bouley Bay, depicts a local 'devil dog' invented as a ruse to keep inhabitants away from coastal footpaths used by smugglers.

It is difficult to know where storytelling ends and myths and folklore begin. There are some examples in this book describing traditions that go back to the distant past. Folkloric characters such as Jack-in-the-Green (Hastings, page 53) and the Straw Bear (Whittlesey, page 125) are inextricably linked to pubs and ale drinking. Even the Gremlin, that mischievous goblin-like creature responsible for a million mechanical faults and breakdowns – and rekindled in J.K. Rowling's *Harry Potter* series – owes his name to a brand of beer. It's a corruption of Fremlin's Beer (brewed in Kent until the 1970s) and the letter G from the Brothers Grimm (the sibling fairy tale authors). The little devil's name was coined by RAF bomber crew stationed on India's North-west Frontier (p115, *A Companion to the Folklore, Myths & Customs of Britain*).

On the subject of myths and folklore, in the archives of Walsall Museum Service is a macabre skeletal arm of a child, that was discovered in a local pub. The Hand of Glory, as it is known, was found hidden in a chimney at the seventeenth-century White Hart Inn, Caldmore End (no longer a pub). According to Victorian mythology, burglars used the hand – which is said to have come from the body of a hanged felon and was imbued with mystical powers – to bewitch victims. Once he or she had fallen into a trance, the house was easily robbed. In more superstitious times, I'm sure many a felon believed in this strange talisman. There is also a mummified hand – albeit one with a different back story – in a Salisbury pub, the Haunch of Venison (page 111).

*Shepherd Neame's Jack-in-the-Green ale is brewed for the eponymous festival held in Hastings.*

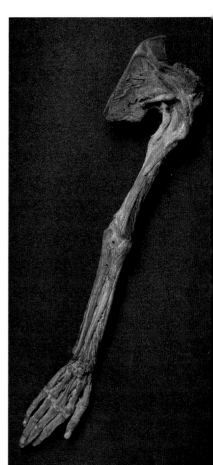

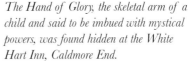

*The Hand of Glory, the skeletal arm of a child and said to be imbued with mystical powers, was found hidden at the White Hart Inn, Caldmore End.*

*This four-wheeled railbus took drinkers to and from Trouble House Halt, a station built specially for the pub of the same name in Gloucestershire. It is pictured in the 1960s*

Sometimes, fact is stranger than fiction. In 1959, the Trouble House Inn (page 122) became that rarest of pubs, having a railway station built exclusively for its drinkers. Unimaginatively named Trouble House Halt, it stood on the Kemble to Tetbury branch line. Trouble wasn't long in coming: in 1964, the toy-like platform fell victim to the railway closures of Dr Beeching. Customers did not take kindly to this. When the last train called, a 'coffin', scrawled with scathing comments and filled with empty whisky bottles, was loaded aboard by 'mourners' in bowler hats – accompanied by a petition for the unpopular British Railways chairman. The mutually interchangeable pub and station name was immortalized in the song *Slow Train*, by Flanders and Swann:

On the main line and the goods siding
The grass grows high
At Dog Dyke, Tumby Woodside
And Trouble House Halt

Pubs seem to reflect their location and those beside water are particularly evocative. Rivers, notably the Thames, are 'liquid history'. I believe its older pubs are able to absorb the past through some form of osmosis. The Prospect of Whitby in Shadwell (page 86) – said to be the oldest hostelry on the river – stands like a beached man o' war that has seen many a sea-dog come and go. Dating from 1520, when it was called the Devil's Tavern, it has been visited by such luminaries as diarist Samuel Pepys, the 'hanging judge' Judge Jeffries, Charles Dickens and, more recently, Richard Burton, Frank Sinatra and Princess Margaret. At low tide, you can descend steps directly onto the foreshore. As the tide recedes, one's eyes are drawn towards the shingle, revealing an astonishing array of artefacts. In a few minutes, I spotted ceramics, earthenware, rusty iron hardware, animal bones, clay pipes, brickwork and terracotta. A different layer of London's past is revealed with each new tide. It's not surprising, as this was once the city's – and England's – most important highway.

Though today's river traffic is busy – in the time it took to drink a pint, I saw tourist boats, commuter catamarans, tugs towing barges of London's rubbish, police hurrying along in a high-speed rib and a restored Thames sailing barge – though this was nothing compared to centuries past. Then, the Prospect would have witnessed an endless procession of vessels large and small, the water being almost choked with sailing ships. Rowing in-between them there were passenger ferryboats, floating general stores ('bumboats'), with the occasional purl-man in a decrepit row-boat, proceeding to the accompaniment of a bell, to attract customers' attention. One of the pubs' main competitors until the late eighteenth century, these vendors would deliver jugs of purl (ale infused with wormwood from the marshes) direct to crews on board vessels.

The hour or so I spent in and around the Prospect was an epiphany, of sorts. I saw a pub that is comfortable with its past, yet busy and popular with today's customers. Where else but the pub can anyone engage with Britain's history and with a cross-section of society too, in such a social setting? Several other Thames-side pubs are featured in these pages, as are further interesting

*England's last official executioner, Harry Bernard Allen, was landlord of this pub in Middleton, Greater Manchester, in the 1960s.*

ones along the mighty Severn. That river had a similar role as an important highway for goods and the beer houses, or 'mug houses' as they were then known, played a key role in refreshing and supporting bow-hauliers. The remote Camp House (page 51), one of my personal favourites, has been run by the same family for eighty years. It oozes history, sells a lovely pint of Batham's Best Bitter and survives against the odds. (It is off the beaten track and sometimes has to close, when flooded by the unpredictable river.)

It is sad that so many pubs have closed in the last decade. The tide may have turned in 2019, however, when there was a net increase of 315 pubs, bringing the total to 39,130 (according to the Office for National Statistics). Closures of traditional and heritage examples are continuing, however. A few I had intended to feature closed during the course of research for this book. Among them was the Woodman in Middleton, Greater Manchester. This was once notable for being run by England's last official hangman, Harry Bernard Allen. He jointly holds the dubious honour of having carried out Britain's last hanging before the death penalty was abolished. (Many think that position is held by the better-known Albert Pierrepoint, who was also a publican, but he resigned in 1956.) Mr Allen, who died in 1992, aged eighty-one, ran a number of Lancashire pubs. He was landlord at the Woodman, a former

Whitbread's hostelry, from 1962-5 and carried out his last hanging for the Home Office whilst there, in August 1964. The guilty party was Gwynne Owen Evans and the location was Strangeways Prison, while Evans's accomplice was simultaneously paying the ultimate penalty at HMP Walton ('Harry had the regulars hanging on his every word', *Manchester Evening News*, 6 April, 2006). The pub started as a silk weaver's cottage, becoming a hostelry in the late 1800s. Various extensions changed the place considerably but it still boasted a well-used dartboard and snooker table, and served a fine pint of Guinness, when it closed in 2019.

Closures of well-run pubs are still the exception. To doomsters claiming that quirky, community-hub pubs are dead or dying, I refer them to three I visited during two days in the Peak District. Not only were they a rich source of stories and humour, they were also busy and thriving – two even without the (perceived) advantage of a food menu. That trip, using a combination of public buses and my Brompton folding bicycle, was also one of the most enjoyable short breaks I've ever had. Which goes for several multi-pub jaunts over the years.

The first establishment was in Bonsall, a straggly hilltop village near Cromford. The Barley Mow (page 30) is renowned for its annual Hen Racing World Championships. Hens wander along

*Bar-skittles being played at the Quiet Woman, Earl Sterndale, whose name hints at an extraordinary story.*

the road outside, while the beer variety inside includes several from its own Chickenfoot Brewery. I started with a pint of SeshHen before moving onto a Great BritHen. I made friends with one of the two dogs (a spaniel called Cocoa) and chatted to locals, who clearly coveted their hostelry. The following day, I found the Quiet Woman in Earl Sterndale (page 41), amid the wild landscape of the High Peak and with more peripatetic hens. There was no food – unless you count a lunchtime pork pie – and no mod-cons, but I enjoyed conversations with the long-term licensee and two elderly locals, who spoke in a broad dialect. While trying to explain why the pub has such an extraordinary name, they were also playing two games simultaneously: bar-skittles and dominoes. Who says men can't multi-task?

The third pub on my trip was the New Inn in Flash. I felt a sense of achievement cycling there as it is, apparently, the highest village in Britain (1519ft). So the New Inn (page 47) must be the highest village pub. The remote village once had a reputation for illegal activities, including cock-fighting and counterfeiting. It's where the expression 'flash money' comes from. Though the inn sign was indecipherable – I was told a new one would be going up in a few days – there was a notice above the door, clearly asserting 'Diane welcomes you to the madhouse.' A placard inside, dated 1921, described the village's Tea Pot Club. Not a W.I. group but 'a strong and wildly esteemed Sick and Burial Society.' As the place had just opened, there were no other customers but two large dogs awaited attention. One greeted me with such enthusiasm that my beer, a moreish microbrewery ale from Macclesfield, sloshed over my trousers. Within a few minutes, the empty bar had filled up as locals piled in – seemingly from nowhere. Soon, they were three deep at the bar. It turned into an evening full of laughter and lots of ale was consumed. I barely remember that downhill, wobbly, starlit ride to my bunk-barn bed for the night.

In this chapter, I have discussed the two main types of pub storytelling. The informal ones – often serendipitous and unstructured – that take place between customers; and the staged storytelling events, where people listen to a 'performer' or watch a play. I recently attended an event that fell somewhere between the two. With an affable compere in charge, tales were introduced by professional storytellers but, after a break to recharge our drinks (mine was a Five Points Pale Ale), the second half consisted mainly of appearances by members of the audience. It was like an 'open mic' session, as attended by amateur musicians. The venue was the Camden Head, a trendy boozer on Camden High Street, and the event – on the theme 'True stories of Catastrophes and Calamities' – was staged by a troop called Natural Born Storytellers.

This was an interactive occasion that I found both entertaining and thought-provoking. First, we were asked to write down examples from our own lives, which the compere read out (anonymously) at intervals. When he read my example, there was a hearty laugh from everyone, which was quite empowering. Many of the tales, told by postgraduate storytellers of both sexes, concerned failed romances, drug-taking disasters, confrontations with harmless perverts and embarrassing problems in the toilet department. There was a synergy with stand-up comedy – and lots of laughs were enjoyed – though laughter wasn't the main aim. Particularly moving was the on-call trainee psychiatric doctor working in a stretched NHS, who had to assess which of his patients might be a serious suicide risk. His story was a mixture of reportage, black humour and pathos, delivered in a deadpan way. He drew one of the longer applauses of the evening.

I found it heartening that the venue was full to capacity, and with predominantly young people, listening to – and interacting with – tales told over a few drinks, in a safe environment. Just as our cavemen forbears would have done in prehistoric times. I didn't see anyone distracted by their mobile phone while people were on stage. I think we are all looking for a chance to escape our hi-tech lives and tap into something more primal. The opportunities pubs offer to link human beings with one another like this are precious. One aspect of the hospitality industry that can never go out of fashion.

Pubs are more than just places to drink beer, meet friends or grab a meal. I will go further by suggesting that they have *souls*. I love them as if they are something alive: capricious, secretive, protective, humorous, surprising and, above all, responsive. Let's all use and savour them, or risk losing them.

*Cast members of 'the Lions part' enjoying the Twelfth Night celebrations at the George Inn, Southwark. The traditional event, at London's last galleried inn, includes storytelling, music, dancing and the 'kissing wishing tree.'*

# LOCATIONS WITH FEATURED PUBS

Key to map numbers. These towns and cities appear in alphabetical order in the Gazetteer. Numbers in brackets show the number of pubs featured in each location.

1. Abingdon
2. Aldermaston
3. Alfriston
4. Ambleside
5. Ashleworth
6. Ashurst
7. Atcham
8. Aylesbury
9. Bewdley
10. Bidford-on-Avon
11. Bishop's Castle
12. Blanchland
13. Bolton
14. Bonsall
15. Bournemouth
16. Broughty Ferry
17. Bude
18. Caister-on-Sea
19. Cambridge
20. Cloughton
21. Coxwold
22. Crawley
23. Crich
24. Dundee
25. Dymchurch
26. Earl Sterndale
27. East Dean
28. East Grinstead
29. Edgerley
30. Edinburgh (3)
31. Flash
32. Gloucester
33. Godalming
34. Grain

35. Gravesend
36. Great Leighs
37. Grimley
38. Guildford
39. Hastings
40. Haworth
41. Hedgerley
42. Hempstead
43. Hooe
44. Keswick
45. Kinver
46. Lancaster
47. Leatherhead
48. Leighton Buzzard
49. Leintwardine
50. Liverpool
51. Llanarmon Dyffryn Ceiriog
52. Llanfihangel Crucorney
53. London (24) (NB The locality of each pub is given in the index)
54. Lyminster
55. Maldon
56. Manchester (2)
57. Marford
58. Musselburgh
59. Mytholmroyd
60. Near Sawrey
61. Norwich (2)
62. Oxford (2)
63. Painswick
64. Pangbourne
65. Penallt

66. Perth
67. Peterborough
68. Pickering
69. Preston (Herts.)
70. Prior's Dean
71. Robin Hood's Bay
72. Rye
73. Saffron Walden
74. Salisbury
75. Santon Bridge
76. Seasalter
77. Slad
78. Southampton (3)
79. South Queensferry
80. Steventon
81. Stiperstones
82. Stirling (2)
83. Sweffling
84. Tetbury
85. Wareham
86. Wellingborough
87. Welwyn Garden City
88. Whitehaven
89. Whittlesey
90. Widecombe-in-the-Moor
91. Winchester (2)
92. Windlesham
93. Wisbech
94. Woolpit
95. Worcester
96. Wymondham

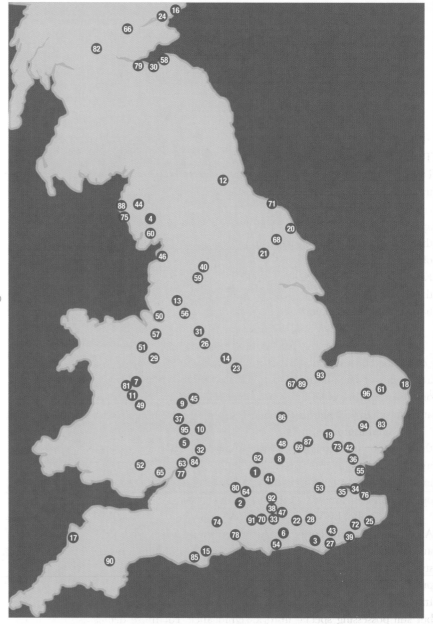

# 2. GAZETTEER OF UNUSUAL PUBS WITH STORIES

THE FOLLOWING PAGES contain a personal selection of Unusual Pubs listed alphabetically by city or town. Entries under London are alphabetical by neighbourhood. All were open to customers at the time of compilation (March 2020). A map of locations appears opposite. This is a subjective list of establishments based on the author's visits. He welcomes comments, including suggestions of pubs to include in future editions, on the Unusual Pubs Facebook page, www.fb.me/Unusualpubs, where updates on this book's content will also be posted, or write to him at bartonwrite1@gmail.com.

## Notes

All establishments are licensed to sell alcohol. Where cask conditioned beer is available it is referred to as 'real ale'. Where the availability of meals is mentioned this may only be on certain days or at certain times. All information is given purely for guidance and may change at short notice.

Some establishments, particularly those in rural areas, close in the afternoon or keep limited hours. Others may close temporarily in winter. Also the coronavirus crisis of 2020 will affect the pub industry for some time. In all cases, readers are advised to check opening times before travelling any distance.

ABV is Alcohol by Volume. CAMRA is the Campaign for Real Ale, an independent, consumer-run organization, founded in 1971 and committed to supporting Britain's pubs and unique brewing style. Where the National Inventory is mentioned, it refers to pubs selected for CAMRA's National Inventory of Historic Pub Interiors. The Regional Inventory covers pubs of lesser intactness but still possessing special historic significance. For more details visit www.camra.org.uk, tel. 01727 867201.

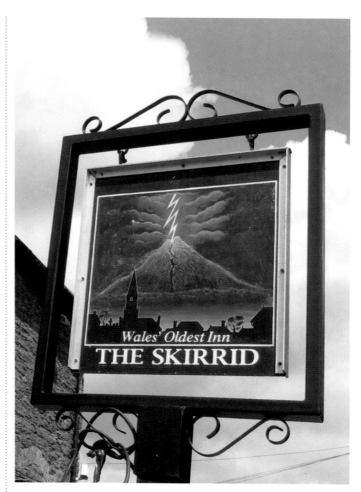

*'Wales' oldest inn' – a former court and place of execution (page 66).*

## ABINGDON, OXFORDSHIRE

### Election of a mock mayor

### *Brewery Tap*

*A newly elected Mayor of Abingdon's Ock Street is taken on a parade along his thoroughfare, from the Brewery Tap in the background.*

Every year since 1700, the people of Ock Street in this Thames-side town have 'cocked a snook' at officialdom and elected their own mayor. The Brewery Tap is the focal point on election day (the Saturday nearest to 19 June) when the winner is announced and feted. With help from Abingdon Traditional Morris Dancers, the celebrations revolve around several drinking establishments, but the fun begins and ends here. The flagstone-floored pub is now free-of-tie but filled with memorabilia of the long closed Morland's Brewery. I enjoyed a party atmosphere and an excellent selection of ales. Animal's Giraffe; West Berkshire's Magg's Magnificent Mild and Vale's Stop Messing About were among the six ales and several ciders on handpump. My favourite was the fruity bitter, Abingdon Bridge (ABV 4.1%) locally brewed by Loose Cannon.

Several nooks and crannies, including a stately, wood-panelled dining room, feed off the main, L-shaped bar. Outside, in a compact courtyard, the mayor's sedan chair, festooned with floral garlands, awaited its new incumbent. It was resting on four empty beer casks. At the appointed time, following some spirited dancing, the winning candidate was announced to a rousing cheer. It was sixty-seven-year-old retired undertaker Harry Knight, who is also a dancer with the Abingdon Morris side, and a dab-hand at the melodeon. After a few proclamations, Harry sat in the floral chair, was raised to shoulder height by some burly men, for a procession along the main street. Then it was back to the serious business of drinking and partying.

This is one of England's last remaining 'mock mayor' ceremonies. The mayor's regalia includes the same ox horns and skull, and wooden drinking chalice, that have been handed down for generations. It was an argument over animal horns during a charity ox-roast in 1700 that began the tradition. Though opponents are often said to 'cross swords', Abingdon men apparently do it with horns. Meals served; accommodation; regular live music; dog friendly.

*Brewery Tap*, 40-42 Ock Street, OX14 5BZ. Tel. 01235 521655. www.thebrewerytap.net

## ALDERMASTON, BERKSHIRE

### Burning the candle at one end

### *Hind's Head*

I joined the Lord of the Manor and the Rector, with the candlestick, in the Officers' Mess. No, this wasn't a game of Cluedo but the start of one of England's last candle auctions. It has taken place in this village – best known for the nearby RAF Bomber Command airfield – every three years for more than two centuries. The venue is this former coaching inn, dating from the seventeenth century. The female Rector called the room to attention and a

*Aldermaston's Lord of the Manor gazes at the all-important candle, as the Rector takes bids, during the Candle Auction of 2019, at the Hind's Head.*

Also unusual is the jail house: a curious, brick-built lock-up at the rear. It was last used in 1865, when the unfortunate inmate burnt himself to death attempting to keep warm.

This is a Fuller's house (formerly Gales, and Adams, when it was called the Pack Horse) and I enjoyed a full-bodied Gales HSB (ABV 4.8%), followed by a hoppy, citrusy Fuller's Fresh Tracks (4.6%). The brewer's London Pride and Santa by the Surf were also on handpump. The interior has been modernized; there is a range of cosy drinking areas and the main bar features a wood-burner, piano and wood floors. There is an attractive garden and board games are available. Accommodation, meals, ambient music, dog friendly. The next candle auction (the first was in 1815) takes place in late 2022.

*Hind's Head*, Wasing Lane, RG7 4LX. Tel. 0118 971 2194. www.hindsheadaldermaston.co.uk

## ALFRISTON, EAST SUSSEX
### Smugglers and pilgrims
### *Star Inn*

tallow candle, with a horseshoe nail inserted an inch below its wick, was lit. The bids came in thick and fast for the lease of Church Acre, a spot of grazing land in Fisherman's Lane. Bidding continued as the candle flame burnt lower. Two churchwardens sucked nervously on their ceremonial clay pipes (the proceeds are for church funds). Suddenly, the flame flickered and the nail dropped from its precarious perch, just as the bidding reached £570. It was over for another three years, though it seemed the night's celebrations had only just begun. The audience, sipping complimentary glasses of rum punch, chatted animatedly. 'It's more fun than a quiz night,' said one. 'Did you know this is the origin of the phrase "you could hear a pin drop"?' said another. Candle auctions are centuries old and were once common – they began for the sale of tea and other ships' cargoes – but now only two others remain. The Aldermaston History Group is proud to maintain the tradition in this Grade II listed inn. It's easy to spot, thanks to its rooftop cupola, topped with a fox weathervane.

A few winters ago, a friend and I enjoyed lunch and a pint beside the blazing fire in this ancient, timber-framed inn, being regaled by locals with stories of the village's smuggling past. Mist swirled around outside and, by the time we left, we couldn't see more than a few yards ahead. I felt the ghosts of the notorious Alfriston Gang were with us that afternoon, conniving to discourage strangers in their 'manor'. Two centuries ago, it was heart of a smuggling route, receiving contraband landed at Cuckmere Haven, then carried along a cart-width track, to be secreted around the village. Then, almost everyone, and certainly every hostelry, was in on the act. The gang was led by Stanton Collins and met here and in the nearby George – until those establishments became too respectable. His father ran a butcher's and beerhouse opposite (then called Market Cross House, it is now Ye Olde Smugglers

*The Star Inn, Alfriston dates from 1520 and some say it is even older.*

Inne. A labyrinthine former hiding place, it is worth a visit). The Star pre-dates that era by a few hundred years, dating from either 1450 or 1520 (Bruning and Paulin, *Historic English Inns*). It began as an inn for pilgrims, called the Star of Bethlehem, run by the monks of Battle Abbey.

The beams are resplendent with religious carvings: St George, St Julian, serpents, a bear and lion among them. The quarry-tiled front bar boasts a Tudor fireplace and, if you can't bear to leave, accommodation is available. Among the local ales served on my visit, I enjoyed a Long Man Best Bitter, with Beachy Head Beachy Original also on hand-pull. The village is good pub-crawl territory and walkers will find it an ideal refreshment stop when trekking the South Downs Way and Vanguard Way. Garden.

**Star Inn**, High Street, BN26 5TA. Tel. 01323 870495.
www.thestaralfriston.co.uk

## AMBLESIDE, CUMBRIA
### A 'fowl' deed narrowly averted
### *Drunken Duck Inn*

According to the 'legend of the drunken duck', which has pride of place on the bar wall, this Lake District inn owes its name to a nineteenth-century landlady. One morning, she found her ducks lying dead outside. Though surprised, she was determined that none would be wasted. Gathering up the birds, she began plucking them for the pot, whereupon they quickly regained consciousness. After getting over the initial shock, the woman realised the fowl weren't dead but *dead drunk*. They had been drinking beer that had leaked from a cask into their feeding ditch. Full of remorse, she made knitted jerseys and kilts of Hawkshead yarn for the naked birds, until their feathers started re-growing. Whether you believe the legend or not, the hostelry – which, though extended, retains the simplicity of its farmhouse beginnings – is remarkable for its beautiful location and home-brewed ales. It also has an enviable reputation for Cumbrian cuisine.

*The Drunken Duck Inn is named after tipsy waterfowl that had a narrow escape from the pot.*

I arrived on my bicycle one glorious autumnal morning, having cycled the few miles from Ambleside. It sits in splendid isolation at a quiet crossroads, with outside benches commanding an unbroken view of distant fells. Inside, the contemporary bar's ceiling is heavy with dried hops; the floor is bare boards, while walls are adorned with prints and awards for beer, restaurant and pub. There are six hand-pulls, all offering ales from the Barngates Brewery in the back-yard. Among them were the amber-gold Tag Lag (ABV 4.4%), a hoppy Brathay Gold (4%), while the ruby Red Bull Terrier (4.8%) – winner of a silver in CAMRA's Champion Beer of Britain 2017 – really hit the spot. In the restaurant, which uses local produce, residents were finishing brunch, or taking an early lunch (dinner booking is advised). It almost seemed a pity to leave, but the sunshine beckoned and the Tower Bank Arms (page 96) is a few scenic miles away. Excellent walking in every direction. Meals, accommodation available, dog friendly (but ducks should exercise caution).

***Drunken Duck Inn***, Barngates, LA22 0NG. Tel. 015394 36347.
www.drunkenduckinn.co.uk

## ASHLEWORTH, GLOUCESTERSHIRE
### Landlord helps an escaping monarch
#### *Boat Inn*

Picture the scene: it is 1651 and King Charles II, in disguise and with a price on his head, arrives at this lonely riverside hamlet. He is desperate to cross the swiftly-flowing Severn as he flees from pursuing Roundheads, following his army's defeat at the Battle of Worcester. A cider-house keeper and river-man called Jelf comes to the rescue, rowing him and his loyal supporters across to safety. In gratitude, the King grants the Jelfs the rights to operate a ferry, in perpetuity. That is the tradition told at the Boat and is a likely story – except that it probably refers to the wrong monarch and battle. Charles II *did* attempt to cross the Severn but the few places were closely watched by Parliamentarian patrols. His flight to the

*This rustic corner of the Boat Inn, Ashleworth includes photos of its river ferry, which last ran the 1950s. The licensee still has the right to operate one.*

coast was probably farther east. According to author and historian Brian Martin, records suggest the landlord's privilege may instead date from around 1460, when Prince Edward of March (later King Edward IV) was fleeing from his Lancastrian enemies during the Wars of the Roses. Certainly, the Jelfs were in the village at that time, as a John Jelf was a leaseholder in 1450.

Today, the hostelry is still secluded. It lies at the end of an ever-narrowing lane, beyond the village with its timber-framed manor house and stone Tithe Barn. I knew I was there as I couldn't go any farther, as the road ends at the river. It is basic, and consequently timeless, with the feel of a place that has been in the same family for 370 years. Or 550, depending on which story you follow.

The Jelf family still own the property but no longer run it – that honour goes to an enthusiastic local, Ian Lock, who holds the lease. He told me he also has the right to run the ferry if he wanted to. A chain once belonging to a chain ferry (it was washed away before World War I) languishes in his shed. A punt was then pressed into service for occasional passengers – and flocks of sheep – until the 1950s. Then it, too, was retired. I noticed a launch 'moored' in the driveway but that is mainly for emergency use, during regular floods, which permeate the building. 'I have known the water rise up to here,' said Ian, placing his hand at chest height. 'That's why we have quarry-tiled floors and rush matting, making it easier to wash everything down when the river invades.' A flood gate beside the road and a raised bank along the river indicate that it is a constant battle. On an early spring day, there is a steady stream of cyclists (NCN Route 45) and walkers taking a break from the Severn Way path, with a queue forming at the narrow bar counter. A choice of three local ales, served from the cask (more in summer), was tempting (Bewdley Brewery's Worcester Way, at 3.6% ABV and Beaulieu, at 4.2%, though I opted for North Cotswold Jumping Jack, 3.9%). Several farm ciders and a perry were available. A compact pub, with simply furnished rooms opening off a narrow corridor. A bevy of awards, from CAMRA and others, is lined up above a cast-iron range and bread oven, in the main room. There is a lounge and dining room too, with a rustic lean-to providing extra space. Outside seating beside the river. Meals, dartboard, mooring. Parking is limited; arrival on foot, or by boat or canoe, is much more fun.

**Boat Inn**, The Quay, near Gloucester, GL19 4HZ.
Tel. 01452 700272.

## ASHURST, WEST SUSSEX
### Favoured haunt of Belloc, Olivier and McCartney
### *Fountain Inn*

*The Fountain Inn, where four friends drank two gallons of ale between them, in Hilaire Belloc's* The Four Men – a Farrago.

'When you have lost your inns, drown your empty selves, for you will have lost the last of England.' This oft-used quote is by Hilaire Belloc, Anglo-French writer (and beer and pub enthusiast) of the early twentieth century. The pub not only featured in his book *The Four Men – a Farrago* but was also actor Laurence Olivier's local and the location used by Paul McCartney for the video accompanying his 1980 hit, *Wonderful Christmas-time*.

Belloc's book, published in 1912, describes his journey on foot across Sussex, from the George Inn at Robertsbridge, via a succession of other hostelries (many still open) in the company of three men: the Sailor, the Poet and the ageing Grizzlebeard. These friends are figments of the author's own character at different times. Accompanied by poems, sketches and a hand-drawn map, the farrago celebrates a county he loved dearly. The walkers consume two gallons of Steyning ale from the Fountain Inn, which they reach on day three of their five-day trek. Returning from the bar, the Sailor announces 'The Fountain runs, but not with common water. It shall become famous among Fountains, for I shall speak of it in rhyme.'

Despite its links with the famous, the Grade II listed pub, which started as a farmhouse, remains a cosy local and a classic one. There are low ceilings, oak beams and a flag-stoned bar at its heart. In this front room, with its inglenook fireplace and blazing fire, Sir Laurence Olivier's portrait hangs in a corner. Here was the seat of Ashurst's most famous resident. Harvey's Sussex Best from Lewes is the regular ale but there are also two changing guests, often local ones (Bedlam Golden and Dark Star Hophead on my visit) as well as a gin menu. Meals are served, with a restaurant extension provided for diners. Bar snacks include homemade Scotch eggs and sausage rolls. An old barn features a skittle alley. There is plenty of seating in a beautiful garden. It contains a duck pond (complete with beach and deckchairs), a Wendy house for children and a shepherd's hut, the latter offering rustic overnight accommodation.

I chose this quote from *The Four Men* (p123):

For inns are as men and women are, with character and fate infinitely diversified, and to one an old man goes for silence and repose, to another a younger man for adventure or isolation… So there are inns coquettish, inns brutal, inns obvious, inns kindly and inns strong – each is for a mood.

I'm not sure which adjective fits the Fountain, but I certainly left feeling happy and carefree. Meals, dog friendly, real fire, skittles.

***Fountain Inn***, Horsham Road, BN44 3AP. Tel. 01403 710219. www.fountainashurst.pub

## ATCHAM, SHROPSHIRE
### Mad Jack's final port of call
### *Mytton & Mermaid Hotel (formerly Talbot Arms)*

This Grade II listed former coaching inn is more akin to a mansion than a pub. Situated 2 miles from Shrewsbury, overlooking the River Severn and the entrance to Attingham Park (a National Trust stately home), it was once a posting house on the route from London to Ireland. When rail travel superseded coaches, it closed to become a residence. Formerly called the Talbot, then the Berwick Arms, it was purchased and reopened in the 1930s by architect Sir Clough Williams Ellis. Known for his Italianate village, Portmeirion in Wales, it was he who coined the present

*The Mytton & Mermaid Hotel was calling point for 'Mad Jack' Mytton's funeral cortege. The eccentric aristocrat squandered his fortune but there was enough left for a respectable wake.*

name. The Mermaid in the title comes from the crest of his Portmeirion Hotel, while Mytton is the name of a local squire, 'Mad Jack' Mytton (1796-1834). He has gone down in history as one of our most eccentric aristocrats. After his life ended in a London debtors' prison, his body rested here on the return for his funeral. Hundreds of people attended – this man's reputation was larger than life.

Jack was the master of wanton excess, who rapidly squandered his inherited fortune on gambling and other vices, and died young. After being expelled from Westminster School, he excelled at sport, particularly hunting (he sometimes rode naked). He was married twice – his first wife died and the second ran away. He bought his way into parliament with £10 bribes, though hardly ever attended; and reputedly drank eight bottles of port daily. He kept many horses – his favourite being allowed to roam inside his house – along with hundreds of foxhounds and gundogs. He fought his bulldog with bare fists. Among his menagerie of exotic pets, Mr. Mytton rode a bear into his drawing room wearing full hunting costume; and tried to cure hiccups by setting his shirt alight. He even attempted to vault over a tollgate with a horse and carriage. Whether any of these antics took place at or around this inn is not recorded.

The three-storey, four-star hotel is a spacious venue, appealing to a wide age range of customers. Though the restaurant and function rooms are often busy with celebrations, the large wood-floored bar, with its wood-burner, is popular with those who merely wish to relax with a drink. I had a choice of three real ales, including the refreshing Salopian Shropshire Gold (ABV 3.8%) and Hobsons Old Prickly (4.2%); there was also Weston's Rosie's Pig cider. It is surrounded by well-kept gardens, one of which sweeps down to the river and a former highway bridge, built in 1768. There is a covered courtyard reached through a grand stable arch, with a mermaid statue as its focal point. Ambient music, regular live music, accommodation.

***Mytton & Mermaid Hotel***, SY5 6QG. Tel. 01743 761220.
www.myttonandmermaid.co.uk

## AYLESBURY, BUCKINGHAMSHIRE
### Where Henry VIII courted and Cromwell rested
### *King's Head*

Ale and history go hand-in-hand here, in the heart of this old market town. An inn since the fifteenth century *(circa* 1455), in recent times the King's Head has become the 'tap' for one of the

*Chiltern Brewery beers 'from the wood' are lined up in the bar of Aylesbury's King's Head, a historic coaching inn owned by the National Trust.*

country's pioneering microbreweries. Entered through one of two arched gateways, it boasts oak beams and a cobbled courtyard, complete with stables. One can easily imagine it being busy with stagecoaches, and their passengers and horses. The building is in the care of the National Trust. Built as a guest house for the local friary, or as a Guildhall – historians cannot agree on which – the manor, and hence the inn, passed to the Boleyn family in the sixteenth century. There are claims that Henry VIII stayed here while courting Anne, destined to be one of his ill-fated wives. The town saw an outbreak of fighting early in the Civil War and, according to Bruning and Paulin in *Historic English Inns*:

> Oliver Cromwell found it a convenient resting-place on his many campaigns. It was here he received the thanks of Parliament after his victory at Worcester in 1651…the room he is said to have used can be seen.

A helpful barman pointed it out from the courtyard, since much of the building is currently closed to the public. This includes a spacious and lofty hall. Again, its stone-mullioned window can be observed from outside. Peeping through a locked door, I was able to see the window's stained glass coats-of-arms of Henry VI, and others, gloriously back-lit.

An area that is open is known as the Farmers' Bar, sporting beams, wonky walls and low ceilings. A contemporary bar counter occupies one corner, with a chalk board indicating the ales served – seven Chiltern Brewery ones on my visit, along with guests from Fallen Brewing and Dorking Brewery; and Orchard Pig cider. When I visited, three of Chiltern's beers were being served from wooden casks. This was an unexpected treat, especially the Chiltern Black (ABV 3.9%), a porter with distinct whisky notes. Wines from the Rothschild Estate are served. Meals, outdoor seating (in courtyard).

Nearby: There's a bronze sculpture of David Bowie, in Market Square. The iconic singer launched his character Ziggy Stardust in Aylesbury.

**King's Head,** King's Head Passage, Market Square, HP20 2RW. Tel. 01296 718812. www.kingsheadaylesbury.co.uk.

## BEWDLEY, WORCESTERSHIRE
### Work deals sealed with mugs of ale
### *Mug House Inn*

In the days before railways, surfaced roads and canals, the River Severn was a major transport artery. Everything from coal and pig-iron to hardware and crockery went by boat and riverside pubs fulfilled a vital role. This one stands on a cobbled quayside (with its own demountable flood barrier) near Thomas Telford's handsome bridge. Barges, or trows, were pulled upriver by brute force. Teams of men, called 'bow hauliers', heaved on ropes attached to chest harnesses. 'Mug houses' such as this were licensed premises where they assembled while awaiting work. Contracts were sealed over a mug of ale – known as 'mugging' – sometimes special mugs were made for the purpose. The standard daily pay was 2s 6d (12½p) plus bread, cheese and ale. There was a penalty of up to three months imprisonment for bow-hauliers failing to keep their side of the bargain: the origin of the expression 'to be had for a mug.' Bewdley's Mug House dates from the early 1800s (it brewed its own beer until 1900), and is one of the last remaining.

Though the inn's interior has changed substantially and extended, its quarry-tiled bar is cosy. It features wood burning stoves, local photographs, a snug area with sofas (and dozens of hanging mugs). There is a single bar counter, stocked with two ciders (Weston's) and five real ales. These were Bewdley Brewery's Worcestershire Way, Hop Shed Frizzle IPA, Wye Valley HPA, Timothy Taylor's Landlord and Purity's Mad Goose. There is riverside seating, while a vine-covered patio provides extra space at the rear and a barbecue in good weather.

The pub features in a poem of 1839 by George Griffith, called *The Devil's Spadeful* after the eponymous local landmark. It tells of the devil's plan to block the Severn and flood the town, using a shovelful of rocks. Satan is thwarted by Tom, a hard-drinking cobbler who meets him one night, on his way home from the pub. Today's walkers have a less stressful time using the Worcestershire

*...ts along the Severn. The Mug*
*...ver's still waters on a summer's*

Way, which passes outside, and the long-distance Severn Way, on the opposite bank. Adjoining restaurant (the Angry Chef), bar meals, accommodation, garden, dog friendly. No parking (use public car parks).

Nearby: Bewdley has a station on the Severn Valley heritage railway.

*Mug House*, 12 Severnside North, DY12 2EE. Tel. 01299 402543.  www.mughousebewdley.co.uk

## BIDFORD-ON-AVON, WARWICKSHIRE
### Villagers drink Shakespeare under the table
### *Frog*

Just 7 miles from his birthplace at Stratford-upon-Avon, Bidford was a drinking haunt of William Shakespeare. In the sixteenth century the villagers were well known for their enthusiasm for ale drinking. They would regularly challenge the people of neighbouring settlements to drinking competitions. According to legend, the Bard accompanied other Stratford locals on one of these binges, though they were quickly out-drunk by the Bidfordians. Will is said to have fallen asleep under a tree after the extended session at the Falcon Inn. When his friends suggested continuing the contest, he replied that he'd had enough, announcing that he had drunk at:

Piping Pebworth, dancing Marston,
Haunted Hillbro', hungry Grafton,
Dudging Exhall, papist Wicksford,
Beggarly Broom and drunken Bidford.

This rhyme is attributed to him, though it didn't appear in print until the *Gentlemen's Quarterly* in 1749. The Falcon, its remaining timber framing covered by stonework, has since closed and been converted to residential use. More recently, other pubs have succumbed so the village, though attractive, is no longer the drinkers' hub it once was. In the riverside Frog, where the above rhyme is proudly painted on an overhead beam, the barman was stoic when I asked if drinking

*Bidford-on-Avon was where William Shakespeare supposedly announced he'd had enough to drink. The Frog is seen from across the river.*

challenges are still held hereabouts. 'No, it's quiet here now, except when we have a live band – there were loads of pubs but now it's just us and the Bull's Head. We get busy in summer, especially outside.' He nodded towards tables on wood decking and a riverside garden facing a medieval stone bridge.

A fire crackled in the wood-floored bar, while locals played a game of darts and others dined. Three handpumps promised ales from Sharp's, Hardys & Hansons and Purity, whose UBU Amber Ale (ABV 4.5%) was hoppy and delicious. The Frog is decorated in a plain, contemporary fashion, though its history is long. Previously, it was called the Boat Inn and, from the 1870s, the Pleasure Boat. Later, I strolled across the ancient bridge to read panels repeating the Shakespeare legend. I continued to the stone-built Bull's Head for a farewell pint of St Austell Tribute, raising my glass to the great pub-crawling poet. Meals, dog friendly.

**The Frog**, 65 High Street, B50 4BG. Tel. 01789 772369.
www.thefrogbidford.com

## BISHOP'S CASTLE, SHROPSHIRE
### Source of the Cleric's Cure – and England['s] 'oldest brewery'
### *Three Tuns Inn*

This seventeenth-century coaching inn is the brewery tap [of] Britain's oldest licensed brewery. Perched at the top of this isolate[d] town, they sit side-by-side or, to use the words of Lonely Planet'[s] online guide, [have] 'been rolling barrels of nut-brown ale across the courtyard since 1642.' It is a proud survivor: in the real ale nadir of the mid-1970s, the Three Tuns was one of only four home-brew pubs left in the country. Though pub and brewery have been separate businesses since 2003, I found a tempting choice of five of its eponymous ales dominating the bar, including Mild (ABV 3.4%) and Stout (4.4%). My hoppy pint of Cleric's

*The Three Tuns Brewery – England's oldest licensed one – stands cheek-by-jowl with the inn of the same name. The author enjoyed a pint of Cleric's Cure.*

*A thirst-inducing line-up of ales on the bar of the Three Tuns Inn.*

Cure (5%), did not disappoint. Its name originates from a letter sent, in 1899, by the Rev. W. Glenn of Wentnor to John Roberts of the Three Tuns, exclaiming that he (Roberts) '…is the only man who has discovered a cure for agricultural depression.'

The cavernous pub is divided into various sections and, though there is a modern dining extension, wood floors, oak-beamed ceilings, bench seating and large fireplaces predominate. Customers ranged from celebrating groups and couples dining, to locals chatting at the bar. A pair of cyclists from the USA arrived, stopping en route between John O'Groats and Land's End. From several windows one can admire the four-storey brewery tower, built in 1888. Ingredients – malt and hops – are winched to the top and they are transformed as production 'descends', becoming ale at ground level. (While here, visit the Six Bells, a contrasting brewpub at the other end of town.) Dog friendly, meals, occasional live music.

**Three Tuns Inn**, Salop Street, SY9 5BW. 01588 638797. www.thethreetunsinn.co.uk

## BLANCHLAND, NORTHUMBERLAND
### Reaching for the stars
#### *Lord Crewe Arms*

The centrepiece of a picturesque, stone-built village, deep in the Derwent valley, this is an ancient inn. It began as the guest house of Blanchland Abbey in the thirteenth century. Though most of what now remains is Georgian, the abbey's kitchen fireplace and a cavernous, vaulted Crypt Bar are medieval highlights. I enjoyed a pint of Crewe Brew, specially made by Wylam Brewery at ABV 4.2% (two other local ales were also available) in this timeless setting. Almost every book I consulted told me it is haunted. Some talk of a wandering monk in a white habit but most famous is the beneficent spirit of Dorothy Forster. She was the sister of General Tom Forster (a Jacobite who led the unsuccessful rebellion of 1715). She helped him escape from prison, days before a trial that would have led to his execution for high treason. According to legend, she brought him here to lay low before he fled to France.

*The Crypt Bar in the Lord Crewe Arms, Blanchland has medieval origins as an abbey guest house.*

Rather than looking for ghosts, I was captivated by the sky. Stepping outside after dark, I gazed in awe at the stars illuminating the inky blackness. The North Pennines of Outstanding Natural Beauty is officially recognized as 'dark sky' locations. Far from sources of light pollution, the Lord Crewe has capitalized on this with evenings of stargazing. Led by astronomers such as Andy Gray, participants, wrapped in blankets against the night chill, peer through telescopes at stars they seem they can almost touch. As the promise of a suppertime stew and a pint of winter ale beckoned, Andy paused. 'Every atom that makes up the human body is traceable back to those stars,' he said. Thought-provoking stuff. Make that two pints of ale, then. Meals, accommodation, real fires, garden.

*Lord Crewe Arms*, The Square, DH8 9SP. Tel. 01434 677100. www.lordcrewearmsblanchland.co.uk

## BOLTON, GREATER MANCHESTER
### A window for every day of the year
#### *Doffcocker Inn*

Calendar houses, where the architecture is influenced by the number of days, weeks or months in a year, are very rare – certainly in the UK – calendar pubs, more so. This lays claim to being one. According to the *Bolton News* (March 3, 2009), its windows contain 365 panes of glass (the number of days in a year), there are 52 doors (weeks in a year), 28 rooms (days in a four-week month), 12 rooms in the cellar (months in a year) and seven bedrooms (days in a week). Counting the cellar, there are four floors (seasons in a year or weeks in a month). The article continues:

Landlord John Bradford said he does not know why the pub was built in such a way but it fascinates his regulars. 'I've never found 100 per cent proof the pub was designed intentionally as a calendar pub but try telling them lot [the regulars] that. There's got to be something behind it.'

*Look through any window: the Doffcocker Inn is said to contain a pane of glass for every day of the year.*

I confess that my friends and I did not stay long enough to check the newspaper's claims. We did, however, speak to a couple of the customers. They were adamant that the substantial boozer, built *circa* 1900 on the site of an earlier hostelry, is dedicated to the Gregorian calendar. It is a labyrinthine place, very well appointed, with mahogany fittings, picture and dado rails, leaded glass doors and upholstered bench seating. Real ale is from the Joseph Holt's range.

Nearby: With the busy Hope and Anchor opposite, this is a stopping point on the popular Bolton – Horwich pub crawl, including several brewpubs, reached using buses on route 125. Darts and other games, garden, occasional live music.

***Doffcocker Inn***, 780 Chorley Old Road, Doffcocker, BL1 5QE.
Tel. 07827 850225. www.joseph-holt.com

## BONSALL, DERBYSHIRE
### Hen Racing World Championships
*Barley Mow Inn*

I arrived in this attractive hilltop village rather breathless, and to the sound of cocks crowing. Then a couple of hens scampered across the road, a few feet from my bicycle. They were an appropriate welcoming committee. The village is known for its Hen Racing World Championships, held annually since 1892. They take place in a spacious yard on a Saturday in August and are run by the pub. I arrived in time to sample one of the first pints from their appropriately named microbrewery, Chickenfoot. The ales continue this avian theme. SeshHen (ABV 3.9%) was fruity; Great BritHen (4.5%) full-bodied. 'We get about seven hundred people here for the hen racing,' claimed Colette, who runs the pub with husband Mick. 'The birds do their own thing, a few stop to peck the ground or lie-down for a sleep. Some get the hang of it, though the record time over the 60-foot course is less than five seconds.'

*A list of events at the Barley Mow, Bonsall, includes its annual Hen Racing Championships, which draws hundreds of spectators.*

*The Barley Mow Inn's bar features hen-patterned wallpaper, avian beermats and ale from its own Chickenfoot Brewery.*

The whitewashed, stone pub dates from the eighteenth century, when it was used by lead miners. With its beams and bare floorboards, it is compact and cosy. Hen patterned wallpaper, avian beermats and chicken paraphernalia provide decoration. It provides sanctuary for other animals too, particularly dogs. (Well-behaved goats and donkeys as well, according to the website.) It is a community hub, with a French speaking club, poetry and open mic nights and live music, among the regular events. As well as their own brews, there were guest ales from Abbeydale and Bradfield, and eight scrumpy ciders. Colette came out to wish me a safe cycle ride home. Not a problem, everywhere is downhill from Bonsall. Meals, outside toilets, dog friendly, outside seating at front.

**Barley Mow**, The Dale, DE4 2AY. Tel. 01629 825685.
wwww.barleymowbonsall.co.uk

## BOURNEMOUTH, DORSET
### An ill-fated boxer's gym
### *Cricketers*

Entering this homely Edwardian hostelry, I noticed a raised seating area, with a decorative roof, ornate fire surround and glazed wooden cabinets. Originally a billiard room, this area was converted to become the private gym of boxing champion Freddie Mills. In his day, it was fully enclosed and private: people could only enter with permission, a local told me. A fading original sign above the window – 'Freddie Mills Pro-Am Boxing Gymnasium' – is the only reminder. Dating from 1847, refitted in the early 1900s and within walking distance of the railway station, the pub claims to be the resort's oldest. It has plenty of original fittings, including curved mahogany bar counters and bar-backs, etched *art nouveau* windows, tiled fireplaces and candy-twist cast-iron pillars. Even the gents' toilet recalls a past era.

I discussed Freddie Mills, who died in mysterious circumstances, with two chatty locals. I sipped a Timothy Taylor's Landlord (Fuller's London Pride and Woodforde's Nelson's Revenge were on too, plus Westons cider). Born in 1919 in Bournemouth, Mills was world light heavyweight champion 1948-50 and a national celebrity. Following retirement from the ring, he became a promoter and entertainer, appearing in several films. He also ran a London nightclub until his death in 1965. Found shot in his parked car, it was assumed to be murder but the coroner passed a verdict of suicide, which his family has never accepted. He was heavily in debt to a crime syndicate and was making a stand against protection racketeers, according to media reports.

Cricketers is comfortable and homely, with wall-to-wall carpets and upholstered bench seating and chairs. The licensee told me she had been resident for sixteen years. 'I haven't changed anything and hopefully it will remain so long after I'm gone,' she said. It has a place on CAMRA's Regional Inventory. Busy on 'home' days at Bournemouth FC, this being the closest pub. Darts, snooker, folk club, meals (weekends), dog friendly, outside seating.

**Cricketers**, 41 Windham Road, Springbourne, BH1 4RN.
Tel. 01202 551589.

*This room in the Cricketers once contained champion boxer Freddie Mills' ring. Note the clerestory roof.*

## BROUGHTY FERRY, CITY OF DUNDEE
### Help for an escaping Jacobite
### *Fisherman's Tavern*

A slate plaque on the wall of this whitewashed, nineteenth-century public house, close to the swift waters of the Tay, remembers an escaping Jacobite army officer. In 1746, Chevalier de Johnstone was fleeing from the rout of Bonnie Prince Charlie's army at the Battle of Culloden. He was assisted by Mally and Jenny Burn, daughters of the landlady of a local alehouse. The plaque recalls that the girls helped him row to freedom across the Tay (as stated in his memoirs) and that '...should it be my lot to return [to Scotland] I shall certainly be at Broughty expressly to see them.' According to research by Prof. Hugh M. Begg, ferrymen imbibing at the inn were too worried to take the Jacobite themselves. They had earlier been threatened by Hanoverian soldiers on the hunt for fugitives. The two young females were willing to help, however, being described as beautiful and charming. De Johnstone was '...deeply affected with their generous sentiments and heroic courage.' Sadly, there is no evidence the officer ever returned.

The Category C listed building, converted from three fishermen's cottages, has appeared in almost all editions of CAMRA's *Good Beer Guide*. It has low ceilings; the rear lounge has tongue-and-groove panelled walls and an ornate fireplace. There are photos of the local lifeboat and a large maritime chart. The counter has six hand-pulls, with ales from Harviestoun, Eden Mill, Isle of Arran, Belhaven; and a Greene King collaboration with Severn Brewing (Late Hopped Pale, 4.4%) on my visit. A stroll to the pretty harbourside is recommended but don't expect to find a ferry – nor any Jacobite soldiers – these days. Meals served, hotel accommodation, garden, dog friendly, occasional live music, ambient music.

**Fisherman's Tavern**, 10-16 Fort Street, DD5 2AD.
Tel. 01382 775941.  www.belhavenpubs.co.uk

*A slate plaque on the wall of the Fisherman's Tavern recalls an escaping Jacobite officer who sought help in 1746.*

## BUDE, CORNWALL

### Birthplace of the Cornish Giant

#### Tree Inn

Pixies are a tourist icon of Cornwall but this was home to someone at the other end of the size scale. Unlike the pixies, Anthony Payne, *aka* the Cornish Giant, actually existed. Standing 7ft 4 in tall and weighing 32 stone, he was born in the building about 1612, when it was the local manor house (it became an inn in the coaching era) and died there. He was a yeoman and was employed as bodyguard to a Royalist commander, Sir Bevil Grenville. In 1643, Payne was by his master's side when he was killed in battle. A quick-thinking Payne rallied the Cornish troops around the nobleman's young son, proclaiming 'a Grenville still leads you!' They were victorious. By the time the giant died, almost fifty years later, his body was so enormous that part of the house had to be cut away to allow its removal. He is remembered with a memorial stone at St James's church, while a portrait (showing him in his finery) is in the Royal Cornwall Museum.

A cannonball from the Civil War is a feature of the pub, while the restaurant, on the other side of the coaching arch, is partly constructed with beams from shipwrecks. I enjoyed local Cornish ales (there were examples from Skinner's, St Austell and Sharp's) in the bar, with its slate floor, log burner and copper-topped counter. On CAMRA's Regional Inventory, meals, accommodation, regular live music, dog friendly.

*Tree Inn*, Fore Street, Stratton, EX23 9DA.
Tel. 01288 352038. www.treeinn.co.uk

*A tall story: the Tree Inn near Bude was birthplace of Anthony Payne, the 'Cornish giant'.*

*The Never Turn Back recalls a local lifeboat tragedy. It stands just yards from the shore, close to the old and new lifeboat stations.*

## CAISTER-ON-SEA, NORFOLK

### A lifeboat tragedy
### *Never Turn Back*

The pub's unusual name commemorates a disaster that occurred in 1901, when the Caister lifeboat *Beauchamp*, responding to distress signals, capsized on a stormy November night. Nine crewmen died. At the ensuing inquest, the coroner asked if the crew was turning back [from its mission]. Lifeboatman James Haylett replied 'Caister men never turn back.' It stands on the edge of sand dunes, yards from the North Sea; an exhibit inside tells the story. The Grade II listed building, opened in 1957, was designed by the chief surveyor of Lacon's Brewery. It is a pleasing mixture of brick, flint and cobbles and the tower is reminiscent of a ship's wheelhouse. The dramatic location emphasises its stylish period look.

I enjoyed a thirst-quenching pint of Adnams Southwold Bitter after cycling from Great Yarmouth. That Suffolk brewer's Ghost Ship was also available. The pub remains largely as built, with separate public and lounge bars. They share a central, shiplap-panelled servery. Nearby: It is a short walk to both old and new lifeboat stations (not part of the RNLI), where more history is displayed and exercise launches are held monthly, on the first Sunday. On CAMRA's Regional Inventory. Meals, garden, dog friendly.

*Never Turn Back*, Manor Road, NR30 5HG.
Tel. 01493 722697.

## CAMBRIDGE, CAMBRIDGESHIRE

### Where airmen left their mark, and scientists celebrated

### *Eagle*

This busy former coaching inn dates back 400 years. It was worth braving the bustling bar in order to enjoy a slice of history. Among a jumble of panelled rooms, the RAF Bar has a grimy ceiling, undecorated since the dark days of World War Two. Allowing time to adjust to the darkness, my eyes revealed an array of signatures, aircraft names and squadron numbers. The work of young British and American airmen, they were etched or burnt on with Zippo lighters, candles or crayon, during 'R&R' breaks between missions. By way of contrast, a blue plaque explains this was the local used by two scientists who discovered the DNA Double Helix 'secret of life'. In February 1953, Francis Crick announced that he and his partner James Watson, working at the nearby Cavendish Laboratory, had successfully unravelled the way DNA carries genetic information. Ales are mainly from the Greene King range, including the Eagle's own DNA Bitter. Meals, garden, real fire.

*Eagle*, 8 Bene't Street, CB2 3QN. Tel. 01223 505020.
www.greeneking-pubs.co.uk/pubs/cambridgeshire/eagle

*Detail of graffiti etched and burnt onto the ceiling of the Eagle, Cambridge by airmen during World War Two.*

## CLOUGHTON, NORTH YORKSHIRE

### Fit for a Queen

### *Blacksmith's Arms Inn*

*By royal appointment: HM The Queen and the Duke of Edinburgh called into the Blacksmith's Arms for lunch.*

May 20, 2010 is a date they're unlikely to forget at this 250-year-old, stone-built hostelry. That's when Queen Elizabeth II and the Duke of Edinburgh pitched up for a pub lunch and drinks. Sherry for Her Majesty, a half of bitter for him. Their signatures, and the special four-course menu (including salmon with Chardonnay sauce, followed by lemon meringue pie) are framed in the rear bar. Portraits of the Queen are hung everywhere. The staff were proud to show me the chairs on which they sat (marked with a 'Q' and 'P'); an album of the event and the very glass Ma'am drank from, complete with royal lipstick marks. She also witnessed a horse being shod in the adjacent blacksmith's forge from which the inn takes its name. Now non-operational, this was the last in the area. The family-run pub is on land owned by the Duchy of Lancaster so, in a way, all who visit are guests of the Queen.

There are two wood-beamed bars, the front lounge containing upholstered bench seating and decorated with horse brasses and polished copper ornaments. With a wood fire at each end, it must be warm in winter. There is a restaurant, where the royal party dined. There were two Yorkshire real ales on my visit: a tasty Black Sheep Choc & Orange Stout (ABV 5%) and a perennial favourite, Landlord (4.3%) from Timothy Taylor's. Meals on the 'specials' board included steak and stout pie, sea bass and barbequed spare ribs. If you don't have a royal limousine, buses from Scarborough and Whitby stop outside. Dartboard, ambient music, outside seating, dog-friendly, accommodation.

*Blacksmith's Arm*s, High Street, YO13 0AE.
Tel. 01723 870244.   www.blacksmithsarmsinn.co.uk

## COXWOLD, NORTH YORKSHIRE

### Tristram Shandy's watering hole?

### *Fauconberg Arms*

Laurence Sterne, author of the bizarre and rambling *The Life and Opinions of Tristram Shandy, Gentleman,* eulogized this moorland village, where he was vicar in the 1760s. He would have known the sturdy, stone-built inn – though under its previous title of the Bellasis Arms – as it dates from the seventeenth century. An alehouse stood on the same site centuries before (p226, Bruning and Paulin, *Historic English Inns*). With stone-flagged floor, heavy joists and yawning hearths, the interior is enhanced with horse brasses, clocks and comfortable furniture. The lounge bar overlooks an attractive main street, while the Oak Room at the rear offers fine views of the Hambledon Hills. Sterne lived at nearby Shandy Hall, which is open to visitors in summer, thanks to the Laurence Sterne Trust. There, you can discover more about this literary giant as well as Tristram's bawdy, satirical and scandalous tales of his family circle.

Four Yorkshire ales were available, including Hambleton Session Pale and Wold Top Wold Gold, along with real cider. It was a joy to sit with a pint beside the log fire, chuckling to myself over Mr Shandy's adventures – and recalling Steve Coogan and Rob Brydon's attempt to film this essentially un-filmable autobiographical novel – in *A Cock and Bull Story* (2006). There is a well-appointed restaurant. Bar meals, accommodation, dog friendly, garden.

*Fauconberg Arms*, YO61 4AD. Tel. 01347 868214.
www.fauconbergarms.com

## CRAWLEY, SURREY
### On a roll at the World Marbles Championship
### *Greyhound*

*Overlooked by video cameras and men with clipboards, a competitor takes his turn in the World Marbles Championship at the Greyhound.*

The game of marbles is taken very seriously here. Especially on Good Friday, when teams come from home and abroad (notably Germany, these days) to compete in the World Marbles Championship. It is handy, therefore, that the spacious, 1930's-built roadhouse is just a short bus or taxi ride from Gatwick Airport. The competition has been held here since 1932, though its history goes back much further. Though I visited at the start of the wettest Easter for years, the inclement weather didn't dampen spirits. A packed schedule of games was played, starting mid-morning, on two permanent outdoor rings, kept carefully dusted with sand. The tournament is officiated by the British Marbles Board of Control, with contestants taking turns using their 'tolley', or shooting marble, to knock 25 red marbles out of the ring. It's all about a keen eye and a deft flick of the right thumb. In 2018, eighteen teams were competing: The Black Dog Boozers doing battle with the Johnson Jets and, after a nail-biting final, the Saxonia Globe Snippers claimed the Friary Meux Challenge Trophy. Then everyone adjourned to the bar to talk 'shooters' and 'taws' and complain about 'cabbaging'.

One bar was reserved for competitors, with a giant board showing the progress of the tournament, as teams moved through

CRAWLEY ARTS COUNCIL

PLAYED ON GOOD FRIDAYS WITH 49 SHOOTING MARBLES (TOLLEYS) ON THE RING, THE WORLD MARBLES CHAMPIONSHIP STARTED HERE IN 1932. REPUTEDLY THE KNOCK-OUT GAME BEGAN IN QUEEN ELIZABETH'S REIGN (1558-1603) AS A DECIDER BETWEEN TWO MEN FROM SURREY AND SUSSEX TO WED A TINSLEY MAIDEN.

THE GREYHOUND

*Plaque at the Greyhound, Tinsley Green.*

the heats, while the other was overflowing with supporters and spectators. Two real ales were served: the house beer, Marbles (ABV 3.9%) and London Glory (ABV 4%), both from Greene King. On the days when no games are taking place, customers can view a gallery of historical championship photos, and there's an array of plaques on the outside wall, marking the game that is said to have begun in Queen Elizabeth I's reign. One of them, a shiny bronze, commemorates Sam Spooner, 'the grand old man of marbles'. A local cowman, he lived most of his life at Tinsley Green and, when marbles were revived [at this pub] in the 1930s, Sam used the same tolley as when he had been champion in the 1880s, some forty-five years before. He died, aged eighty-five, in 1946.

*The Greyhound*, Radford Road, Tinsley Green, RH10 3NS. Tel. 01293 884220. www.greyhoundtinsleygreen.co.uk.

*A tram rattles past the magnificent Red Lion Hotel, which was moved from Stoke and rebuilt, brick by brick, at Crich in 1990.*

## CRICH, DERBYSHIRE
### A moving experience
### *Red Lion Hotel*

Have you ever wondered how to move a pub, brick by brick, a distance of 50 miles? If so, you are in luck: the process is illustrated within. Not only was the Red Lion moved from Stoke-on-Trent and rebuilt here, but most of the work was carried out by National Tramway Museum volunteers. One of the country's finest *Art Nouveau* structures, it is built of terracotta, glazed faience and brick. Threatened with demolition in 1973, due to road improvements, the structure was saved and, since 2001, has been the focal point of the museum's Edwardian street. A variety of preserved trams pass its doors and I was transported to the era when these imposing electric vehicles were an everyday means of transport.

After many years languishing in a field, re-assembly of the hotel's component parts – a three-dimensional jigsaw puzzle – began in 1990. The café-like interior is not the original. This open-plan, slate floored room (with a further space upstairs) has a wood-burning stove and features a wooden bar counter from Nottingham Prison social club. Coloured glass windows are recent. The large lion mounted on the roof is a glass fibre replica of the terracotta original, which sadly did not survive the journey into the Peak District.

At least one real ale is normally available: I was able to choose between Lenton Lane 36 Degrees (ABV 3.9%) and Brampton Golden Bud (3.8%). Handpumps were not in use, ale being drawn directly from casks behind the bar. These are cooled using a combination of an electric fan and jackets containing freezer packs. Open during museum hours only (entrance fee payable). Meals served.

***Red Lion Hotel***, Crich Tramway Village, near Matlock, DE4 5DP. Tel. 01773 854350. www.tramway.co.uk

## DUNDEE, CITY OF DUNDEE
### The 'world's worst poet'
### *Speedwell Bar (Mennie's)*

Though it is known for possessing one of the finest Edwardian pub interiors in Scotland, less obvious is that Mennie's was home to fans of 'the world's worst poet'. Dundee resident William Topaz McGonagall (1825-1902) was a heroic failure as a poet and widely mocked in his lifetime. More recently, according to his biographer Norman Watson, his works were popularized by comedian Spike Milligan, as well as featuring in *Monty Python's Flying Circus*. *Harry Potter* author J.K. Rowling named the character Minerva McGonagall after him. The Dundee W.T. McGonagall Appreciation Society met regularly until the late 1990s. In the bar, I chatted with Linda Geekie, a founder member. The society convened monthly in Mennie's, following closure of a nearby bar bearing the poet's name. 'We even had a couple of AGMs here,

which were like Burns' Night, though less reverential. We invited Spike Milligan to one; he didn't come but fellow comedian Barry Cryer did us proud, he's a great fan. I feel inspired to revive the society. Some of his poetry really wasn't that bad, you know.'

Mennie's, with its glazed partitions, is resplendent in polished mahogany, including the counter and L-shaped bar back. Some of the 150 malt whiskies sold are displayed there. My visit found three real ales: Law Weekender Pils (ABV 5%), Caledonian Deuchars IPA (3.8%), a moreish Stewart Brewing Talini Tangerine IPA (4.8%), plus Belgian bottled choices and Guinness West Indian Porter (6%). Other decorative features include bell-pushes, etched glass panels and an Anaglypta Jacobean ceiling. No wonder it's on CAMRA's National Inventory of historic interiors. The gents' toilet retains its Shanks' 'Odourless' urinals and mosaic floor. I enjoyed friendly conversations in this much loved, busy local. An ironic post-script to the McGonagall story is that the self-styled 'poet and tragedian' was zealously anti-alcohol. His poem *The Destroying Angel* even describes the deliberate destruction of Dundee's pubs. Specifically, those on the Perth Road. Dog friendly, live folk music.

***Speedwell Bar***, 165-167 Perth Road, DD2 1AS. Tel. 01382 667783. www.speedwell-bar.co.uk

*A busy corner of the Speedwell Bar, aka Mennie's, where customers recall the 'world's worst poet.'*

## DYMCHURCH, KENT

### A shipping disaster, and the 'Day of Syn'

### *City of London (formerly Seawall Tavern)*

It was a mighty storm that blew in from the English Channel in 1775. It lifted a ship clean out of the sea and hurled it against the Seawall Tavern. Many people were killed, and the building badly damaged. The ship was called the *City of London*. Its timbers were used in the repair of the pub, which changed its name to that of the ill-fated vessel, in memory of the victims. Author Russell Thorndike featured the tavern, using its original name, in his *Dr Syn* novels about a local vicar who is a smuggler by night. Tales of smuggling run through every street, alleyway and pub of this town on the edge of Romney Marsh. It was wild, thinly populated countryside, where smuggling was carried on with little fear of arrest. The locals are so taken with Thorndike's stories that they bring the salty characters, led by the evil Scarecrow, back to life every two years, with a 'Day of Syn' on August Bank Holiday.

There are patrols of Redcoat soldiers, skirmishes and arrests of smugglers and battles on the beach between the opposing sides. The whole town enters into the spirit.

I arrived at this twin-level pub on carnival day, in time to sample a commemorative beer from the Romney Marsh Brewery, Day of Syn Scarecrow Ale (ABV 4.4%). It was most satisfying, as was Romney Marsh Gold (4.1%). Canterbury Ales Golden Bitter (3.9%) and Wychwood Hobgoblin (4.5%) were also on hand-pull. Characters in eighteenth-century costume were milling about and, incongruously, a band was blasting out the Kinks' *You Really Got Me*, inside the packed bar. The canopied terrace, on the seaward side, was also busy with customers, while the downstairs bar, reached via steps on the *outside* of the pub, was more sedate, being used for dining. Meals, dog friendly.

Nearby: The sea wall is good for a breezy stroll after a beer. The Ship Inn, at 118 High Street, dates from 1530 and had four real ales.

*City of London*, 68-70 High Street, TN29 0NL.
Tel. 01303 873979.  www.cityoflondondymchurch.co.uk

*Participants enjoying the biennial 'Day of Syn' at the City of London tavern in Dymchurch.*

## EARL STERNDALE, DERBYSHIRE
### The tale of Chattering Charteris
### *Quiet Woman*

While earning no points for political correctness, this is one of the country's more unusual pub names. The time-worn inn sign shows a headless woman walking with a tray of food and drink, with the cryptic motto: 'Soft words turneth away wrath'. There has been a pub at this remote location, in a lovely Peak District village, for 400 years. The woman is said to be 'Chattering Charteris', who tormented her husband through endless scolding, which extended to talking in her sleep. Driven to madness, he cut off her head. The villagers, who seem to have condoned the murder, collected money

*Inn sign for a pub that has a macabre story behind the name: the Quiet Woman in the Peak District.*

for a headstone and inscribed it with a warning to all chatterboxes (p112, *The Most Amazing Places of Folklore and Legend in Britain*).

The low-beamed, quarry-tiled hostelry is furnished with wooden settles and a centuries-old undertaker's table. It also boasts a real fire, piano and traditional pub games, including darts and snooker in a separate games room. I enjoyed a pork pie and supped a Wainwright Golden (ABV 4.1%, other ales were Bradfield Farmers Stout and Marston's Bitter) while chatting with three locals who were alternating between games of bar skittles and dominoes. Who said men can't multi-task? As well as ale, the landlord sells free-range eggs, his hens demonstrably scratching around outside. It doubles as the local post office once a week. On CAMRA's Regional Inventory. Garden, camping.

Nearby: In the heart of the Peak District, this is a good location for walks.

**Quiet Woman**, Off B5053 south of Buxton, SK17 0BU. Tel. 01298 83211.

## EAST DEAN, EAST SUSSEX
### Smugglers ahoy!
### *Tiger Inn*

Thanks to coastal erosion, the settlement of Birling Gap is slowly crumbling into the sea. East Dean, a short walk away, survives intact, this centuries-old hostelry at its heart. Farther inland is the Long Man of Wilmington, a mysterious, giant figure cut into the hillside. He's inspiration for the Long Man Brewery, whose hoppy Long Blonde (ABV 3.8%) was one of six fine ales. I first visited the Tiger Inn after a heavy snowfall, at the end of a cliff walk. A fellow customer made me realise what a fool I had been. 'The cliff edge is hard to define even in good weather, let alone with a snow camouflage,' he said. He explained that smugglers once used to haul up contraband by basket. In 1750, Excise Man Thomas Fletcher fell to his death and, though he may simply have

*The Tiger Inn at East Dean, reached by the author after a frigid cliff walk*

been pushed, it's more likely the bootleggers deliberately moved chalk markers the officers positioned, to indicate a secure path at night. A stumble and fall would be the inevitable consequence. Behind the inn I admired a handsome, bow-windowed house, 'The Dipperays,' built five years after Fletcher's death, for churchwarden James Dipperay. A surprisingly grand residence for a humble church servant, it is claimed Dipperay made a fortune from smuggling.

All but the shortest customers duck their heads on entering the flagstone-floored bar. A delightful place in a sylvan setting. Accommodation, meals, outside seating, dog friendly, real fire.

*Tiger Inn*, The Green, near Eastbourne, BN20 0DA.
Tel. 01323 423209. www.beachyhead.org.uk/the-tiger-inn

## EAST GRINSTEAD, WEST SUSSEX
### The town that didn't stare
*Crown (formerly Commercial Inn and Bar Kuba)*

For seventy-five years, the town was home to the world's most unusual and exclusive band of drinkers. The Guinea Pig Club was made up of Allied airmen who had been injured – badly burned – in World War Two. With often raucous antics, and an anthem that included the line 'we'd rather drink than fight,' it was

*The sign of the Guinea Pig pub, closed in 2007, is now an exhibit in East Grinstead Museum.*

and courtroom added the following century. More recently, the licensed part has been reduced in size. The roomy bar is decorated with poster-sized historical photographs of the town where, for many years, the Guinea Pig Club held an annual 'lost weekend'. It was known as such because of the amount they drank. They also went on morale boosting pub crawls. According to member Tom Cleave, the locals were so welcoming 'you had a job paying for a pint yourself.' Meals, outdoor seating.

Nearby: East Grinstead Museum, Old Market Yard, Cantelupe Road, RH19 3BJ. www.eastgrinsteadmuseum.org.uk.

*Crown*, 35 High Street, RH19 3AF. Tel. 01342 327947. www.crowneastgrinstead.com.

## EDGERLEY, SHROPSHIRE
### All aboard the Flood Bus
### *Royal Hill Inn*

*The Crown in East Grinstead, whose records date from 1502, was among those visited by members of the Guinea Pig Club. Pictured on the town's vintage bus running day.*

a mutual support network for more than 600 aircrew undergoing pioneering medical treatment at East Grinstead's Queen Victoria Hospital. Their facial disfigurements – and weird skin attachments used as part of their treatment – were handled with aplomb, not just by the patients but also by the locals. It became known as 'the town that didn't stare.' Until closure in 2007, the club even had its own pub, the Guinea Pig (the experimental medical techniques used led to the patients being so-called). The original inn sign, painted by P.J. Oldreive, forms part of a permanent exhibition telling the story at East Grinstead Museum.

With records dating from 1502, the Crown was once the town's principal inn and was patronized by Guinea Pig members (as were many local pubs open in the 1940s). Conveniently, its rear entrance is a few paces from the museum. I enjoyed a nutty Harvey's Sussex Bitter (other real ale choices were Timothy Taylor's Landlord and Sharp's Doom Bar) in the company of a wide age range of customers, many enjoying Sunday lunch. The timber-framed inn was largely rebuilt in brick in the late 1700s and a market room

Situated in splendid isolation overlooking the River Severn, this brick and stone-built hostelry dates from the eighteenth century. Its history has been intertwined with that of the river ever since, but if you are not arriving direct from its shore (perhaps as a canoeist, fisherman or walker on the Severn Way), it is well worth seeking out along narrow country lanes. Though extended over the years, the Royal Hill retains its original, quarry-tiled front bar, complete with high-backed settles, and diminutive servery with antique counter, that earns it a place in CAMRA's Regional Inventory.

First owned by a river trader, Samuel Higgins, it refreshed passengers who used a ferry that ran for many years. This was one of the Severnside 'mug houses' where human towing machines, known as bowhauliers, were hired over a mug of ale (see Bewdley, page 25). Like most properties close to the Severn, the pub is affected by regular floods, yet this one has an ingenious way of mitigating the effects on its business. A former French Army amphibious vehicle, built in the 1960s and dubbed the 'flood bus',

*The Flood Bus ready for action outside the Royal Hill Inn, situated near the River Severn at Edgerley.*

## EDINBURGH, LOTHIAN (1)
### A royal game of skittles before the battle
### *Sheep Heid Inn*

Tucked away in Duddingston village, close to its eponymous loch, Holyrood Park and the volcanic outcrop of Arthur's Seat, is this mid nineteenth-century gem. (There was an inn here in the fourteenth, making it one of Scotland's oldest sites of hospitality.) The wood panelled main bar features an Edwardian semi-circular counter, overlooked by a painting of Bonnie Prince Charlie at Prestonpans. His Jacobite troops camped in the village before the Battle of Prestonpans (1745) and the soldiers reputedly played skittles here. Its link with the game actually goes back further. In 1580, James VI of Scotland presented a gift of a snuff box made from a ram's head, to thank the inn for some good skittling (a replica is behind the bar, the original is at Dalmeny House). The extant double lane skittle alley was built in 1882 on the site of a

was purchased by landlord John Bewley and called into action when surrounding roads are underwater. As it can operate in depths up to 5 feet (1.5m), it is ideal for ferrying regular customers. So successful is it that it has also been used to help farmers rescue stranded animals and Shropshire Fire and Rescue Service even expressed interest in borrowing the contraption (*BBC News Online*, 7 March, 2007). A sign, usually displayed in the bar, 'Flood Bus in operation', gives the pub's phone numbers and is placed, when required, where people can safely summon this unusual form of public transport. There are photos of past floods to examine.

Real ales were Salopian Shropshire Gold, Three Tuns XXX and Wye Valley HPA; the latter quaffed whilst sitting alfresco on Ruby's bench. This was placed, in its scenic spot, in honour of a long-serving landlady. On CAMRA's Regional Inventory. Meals, real fires, dog friendly, snooker and darts, outside seating, camping.

***Royal Hill Inn**, SY10 8ES. Tel. 01743 741242.*
*www.royalhill.co.uk*

*Bowled over: the Sheep Heid Inn's skittle alley has been officially named one of Edinburgh's most historic objects.*

stable block. In 2017, it was named one of Edinburgh's 101 most treasured objects (https://edinburgh.org/101). It is used regularly by Trotters Club, founded in 1888 by three journalists and revived in 1943. New players are welcome. A link with royalty remains: in 2016, Queen Elizabeth II called in for supper.

The establishment is popular with diners but drinkers are welcome. I enjoyed a well-kept Inveralmond Lia Fail (ABV 4.7%). Other choices were Orkney Red McGregor and Caledonian Edinburgh Castle. Wide choice of bottled beers, ciders and wines. Courtyard garden, dog friendly.

Nearby: I enjoyed a scenic walk from Edinburgh along the Innocent Railway Path (NCN Route 1), or buses stop within walking distance.

*Sheep Heid Inn*, 43-45 The Causeway, Duddingston, EH15 3QA. Tel. 0131 661 7974.
www.thesheepheidedinburgh.co.uk

## EDINBURGH, LOTHIAN (2)

### A prison and place of execution
#### *Tolbooth Tavern*

The Royal Mile is a remarkable thoroughfare, where history is palpable. The Tolbooth is among its focal points; a sixteenth century stone fortress, with intimidating tower and turrets – and a massive clock. For years, it served as a prison whose conditions were notorious. Prisoners included Covenanters (1661-88) and Royalist soldiers, some of whom daringly escaped from its upper windows (1654). It was also a place of execution: prisoners were hanged or beheaded on gallows erected outside. The 1st Marquess of Montrose (1650) and 9th Earl of Argyll (1685) both suffered this fate. The Tolbooth was an official city entry point, built in the 1590s to collect fees from travellers. The front portion became a tavern only in 1820, with the rear following suit a century later. An arch to the side allowed entry to stage coaches.

I was surprised to find the interior a comfortable and inviting contrast to the frontage, though some stone walls remain bare. There is upholstered bench seating, a raised dining area and carved wooden bar counter. I enjoyed a hoppy, blonde Jarl (ABV 3.8%) from Fyne Ales in Argyll, other options being Caledonian Deuchars IPA and its stablemate Edinburgh Castle. Meals, dog friendly.

*Tolbooth Tavern*, 167 Canongate, EH8 8BN.
Tel. 0131 629 4500. www.tolboothedinburgh.co.uk

*Edinburgh's Tolbooth Tavern occupies part of a sixteenth-century fortress on the Royal Mile.*

## EDINBURGH, LOTHIAN (3)
### Where Burns dreamed and Burke and Hare stalked
#### *White Hart Inn*

Situated on the cobbled Grassmarket, beneath Edinburgh Castle, this is said to be the city's oldest inn. It dates from 1516, though only the cellars survive from that date. Above ground, the building dates from 1740 (p.235, Anthony Cooke, *A History of Drinking: the Scottish Pub since 1700*.) Executions would be held just to the east and these public events kept generations of publicans busy. A wealth of stories emanate from the inn but I will quote two favourites. Robert Burns, the national poet, spent a week here in 1791, when visiting his lover Nancy Macklehose for the last time. Suitably inspired, he wrote *Ae Fond Kiss*. Famous lines from his poetry are painted along the ceiling rafters, in the wood-beamed bar. The White Hart was

*The sweets of love are washed with tears: the White Hart Inn was used by Robert Burns when visiting his lover for the last time. His quotations are emblazoned across its beams.*

one of the haunts of notorious body snatchers Burke and Hare who, in 1828, roamed this pub – and other local drinking haunts – finding victims to murder, selling the cadavers to Dr Knox at the city's medical school. William Burke was executed for his crimes the following January (William Hare turned King's evidence and was spared the noose). A contemporary account of the hanging is displayed, along with a gruesome effigy. Among other famous and infamous visitors were Oliver Cromwell and William and Dorothy Wordsworth. Ambient music, outdoor seating.

On a raw evening, I found a pint of Belhaven Black Scottish Stout (ABV 4.2%) a perfect accompaniment to a portion of fish pie and vegetables. Other real ales included the brewery's 1719 Pale Ale (4.5%), and Greene King White Hart Best (3.9%).

Nearby: A few doors along is another interesting pub. The Beehive (formerly Beehive Hotel) is on the site of a fifteenth-century inn. Ascend to the first floor to see a macabre feature: the door to the condemned cell at Calton jail, removed at the time of the prison's demolition. Five different ales are served.

***White Hart Inn***, 34 Grassmarket, EH1 2JU.
Tel. 0131 226 2806. whitehart-edinburgh.co.uk

## FLASH, STAFFORDSHIRE
### The highest village pub
### *New Inn*

I needed a pint after reaching this lofty pub (Flash is claimed as the country's highest village – 1518 feet above sea level). I'd cycled there on my Brompton, across miles of wild moorland. As my knees discovered, this folding bicycle isn't designed for hills. New Inn is a misnomer, as the hostelry, fashioned from local millstone grit, has a 250-year heritage. Away from the law's prying eyes and close to the borders of three counties, the village once had a reputation for lawbreaking. It was the haunt of highwaymen and cock-fighting and coin counterfeiting took place. It is said to be the source of the expression 'flash money'.

The pub has been modernized, though in a way that has maintained the atmosphere of a modest country boozer. A new pub sign, announcing 'Britain's highest village pub' in giant letters, sat on the stone floor awaiting erection outside. I preferred the old one hanging outside, soon to be replaced, bearing the peeling portrait of a masked brigand who once 'worked' the area. My first pint, Bosley Cloud (ABV 4.1%) from Macclesfield's Storm Brewing, was enjoyed in the company of two friendly dogs and a few regulars. The pub became busier and livelier as the evening

*The New Inn, Flash, with its old inn sign showing the head of a local brigand. It was once a lawless village.*

wore on – this is a place the locals enjoy, clearly encouraged by another sign, hanging above the bar: 'Diane welcomes you to the mad house.' Ambient music, dog friendly, outside seating.

*New Inn*, High Street, SK17 0SW. Tel. 01298 22941.

## GLOUCESTER, GLOUCESTERSHIRE
### Home of the Sunday School pioneer
### *Robert Raikes' House (formerly Golden Cross)*

Journalists, once known as heavy drinkers, will no doubt raise a smile at the fact that this early newspaper office (the *Gloucester Journal* occupied it from 1758) is a pub. The restored, timber-framed building dates from 1560 and was home to newspaper proprietor Robert Raikes (1736-1811). Also a philanthropist, he is best known as founder of the Sunday School movement, which

*Robert Raikes' House in Gloucester was home to a pioneer of Sunday schools in the 1700s and has been superbly restored.*

started as a school for boys from the slums. Classes were held in the garden, now a courtyard. Tadcaster brewer Samuel Smith restored it at great expense (reportedly, £4.5m) and reopened it in 2008. The restoration is remarkable and the interior, devoid of usual pub clutter, instead reveals bare wattle and daub walls and heavy timber beams. Technical drawings, paintings and the house's distinguished history are displayed. Old Brewery Bitter and other products from the Samuel Smith's range are sold. Meals, traditional pub games.

**Robert Raikes' House**, 38, Southgate Street, GL1 2DR. Tel. 01452 303530.

## GODALMING, SURREY

### The hungry czar
### King's Arms and Royal Hotel

Pubs often claim they have been visited by a celebrity but this establishment has a prouder boast. In March 1698, it was patronized by the czar of Russia and his entourage. Peter the Great stopped for a night when travelling between Portsmouth and London. A plaque presented by the citizens of Moscow on the tercentenary of his visit is displayed outside. A portrait of the giant (he was 6ft 8in, or 2.03 metres tall) hangs in the lobby. The cosy, wood-panelled Czar Bar is another reminder. At Godalming Museum nearby, a curator drew my attention to the menu served to the czar's party. Dinner included five ribs of beef, eight rabbits and one sheep. Breakfast was washed down with three quarts of brandy and six of mulled wine.

For many years, this was one of the town's main coaching inns – it stood on the London to Portsmouth road; Godalming was a popular overnight stop on the two-day journey. Some coaches carried convicts *en route* to transportation. They would arrive around midnight, under armed guard. Chained together, they would take exercise and refreshment in the yard, before continuing to the coast. The lengthy, three-storey frontage, with a distinctive brick pattern, dates from 1753 and conveys the inn's historical importance. Decoration in the labyrinthine bar area includes a stained-glass ceiling dome, cast iron balustrades, an ornate bar-back and period photographs. I was told that redecoration was imminent, so some features may have changed. The 'royal' in the title is thanks to a visit from King Henry VIII and one can only speculate on what he ate. I was able to choose between three local real ales: Tillingbourne Fool's Gold (ABV 4.2%), Dorking Red India (5%) and Hog's Back Little Swine (2.8%). Meals, accommodation, dog friendly, ambient music, garden.

Nearby: The riverside park has a memorial to the radio officer of RMS *Titanic*, Jack Phillips, who hailed from Godalming and was lost in the sinking.

**King's Arms and Royal Hotel**, 22-26 High Street, GU7 1EB. Tel. 01483 421545. www.historicinnz.co.uk/godalming

*Peter the Great of Russia called at the King's Arms Royal Hotel, Godalming in 1698. By all accounts, his party consumed a vast quantity of alcohol.*

## GRAIN, KENT
### Artist William Hogarth 'on the town'
### *Hogarth Inn*

A remote limb of Kent – between the Thames and Medway – the Isle of Grain is an other-worldly combination of marshes, industrial relics and scattered settlements. Shortly before the road ends abruptly, at an ancient church and waterside park, is this Grade II listed inn. It is linked with one of England's greatest artists. William Hogarth (1697-1764), best known for prints such as *A Harlot's Progress*, *Gin Lane* and *Beer Street*, called here in 1732 (when it was known as the Chequer Alehouse, kept by one Goody Hubbard). It was part of a holiday with a difference. The idea of this lads' outing by boat and on foot, where Hogarth was accompanied by four friends, was dreamt up in a Covent Garden pub. A publication describing the trip was illustrated by the artist and published fifty years later. It was written by Ebenezer Forrest and titled *Five Days' Peregrination – Hogarth's Frolic*. The tale involves lots of drinking, eating and high jinks, including various play-fights, using hog dung and pebbles as ammunition. An amusing satire on the aristocratic Grand Tours of the period, it is rather laddish. In the churchyard at Hoo, for example, Hogarth 'untruss'd upon a Grave Rail in an unseemly Manner' (had a bowel motion). This is not a book to give to your mother-in-law.

My friend Richard and I also arrived here after a day's walking, making our final approach on the 191 Arriva bus. A poor substitute for a peregrination, admittedly. The two-roomed pub was divided into a quiet side and noisy side, as the England World Cup team was on television in the main bar. The landlord was ebullient, confirming that Hogarth had indeed dined there, as if he had only left yesterday. Various prints by the artist decorate the walls, and though the inn has been enlarged, aged oak beams and sagging ceilings indicate its late sixteenth-century beginnings. (It spent part of the twentieth as a post office.) Two real ales were on hand-pull – Adnams Ghost Ship and Salcombe Gold – but the pump-clips change regularly. This community-oriented pub has two dart boards and a snooker table indicating it is also sports oriented. We found it agreeable, but Hogarth's party seemed to be in a hurry to leave Grain. Unfortunately, the ferryman was reluctant to set sail and his substitute claimed the wind was blowing too hard. So the friends had to trek across the marshes and flag down a passing boat – using a plank to crawl aboard – the nautical equivalent of hitch-hiking. Outdoor seating.

*Hogarth Inn*, 41-43 High Street, Grain, ME3 0BJ.
Tel. 01634 470932.

*The Hogarth Inn was visited by the eponymous artist on a wild 'peregrination', accompanied by four friends, in the 1700s.*

## GRAVESEND, KENT

### Riverside pub that confounded the Press Gang
### *Three Daws (formerly Three Cornish Choughs)*

Though much altered, this centuries-old maritime pub overlooking the Thames boasts stories of smuggling, hidden tunnels–and the feared Press Gang that forced young men into naval service. Gaining its first licence 450 years ago (1565), it started as a row of cottages erected by ships' carpenters. The freelance nature of its construction meant higgledy-piggledy staircases and nooks and crannies, some of which are still evident. With the adjacent Old Pilot's House (now demolished) it had seven staircases and three tunnels. These provided ample opportunity for men to evade the King's men, aka the Impress Service, which was staffed by determined naval officers. It often used surprise raids on pubs as a way of cornering fit, seafaring males for years of maritime duty. Many of these men never returned home. The inn's warren of diverse escape routes made evading the gangs so easy that, in 1798, the Admiralty ordered the raids should only take place when two teams could work together, 'as so many seamen escape through its tortuous passages.'

The tunnels, none of which are now evident, also provided storage areas for smugglers' contraband, during the Stuart period. In 1780, 80 gallons of illicit Jeneva (gin) was discovered there by the authorities. The Grade II listed pub, a composite of brick, timber and weatherboarding – and, inside, sloping floors and ceilings, exposed brickwork decorated with old prints – stands beside the Town Pier. This, the world's oldest cast-iron pier, is used by the Tilbury ferry. A riverside terrace provides a vantage point for watching it, and the cargo ships plying the Thames. There were six ales: I enjoyed a Marsh Mallow from Romney Marsh Brewery (ABV 3.6%), with other local offerings including Dartford Wobbler (4.3%) and Musket Brewery Powder Burn Porter (5%), plus ales from Dorking Brewery and Adnams. The menu uses Kentish produce (booking recommended for Sunday lunch). Bar billiards, live music, ambient music.

Nearby: The town has lots of historical interest and, for walkers, is starting point of the Saxon Shore Way, which follows the Kent coast.

*Three Daws*, 7 Town Pier, DA11 0BJ. Tel. 01474 566869. www.threedaws.co.uk

*The Thames-side Three Daws, Gravesend, was often raided by the Press Gang but its regulars knew the escape routes.*

## GREAT LEIGHS, ESSEX

### The witch of Scrapfaggot's Green
### *The Castle (formerly St Anne's Castle Inn)*

This well-kept, former Chelmsford Brewery and, later, Ind Coope pub, situated between Braintree and Chelmsford, claims to be England's oldest licensed premises. Though the date of circa 1174, engraved outside, may be optimistic, the place does have a long pedigree. It is shown as St Ann's on a map published in 1675, *Ogilby's Itinerarium Angliae*. In *White's History and Gazetteer of Essex*, it is described as a one-time hermitage, where ale-drinking pilgrims sought shelter on their treks to Thomas à Becket's shrine

*The Castle at Great Leighs stands on the site of a medieval hermitage.*

in Canterbury. Despite a few ageing beams, today's building is more recent. A solitary rock outside piqued my curiosity. A cryptic notice alongside announces it as 'the stone that sealed the grave of the witch of Scrapfaggot's Green.'

*A Companion to the Folklore, Myths & Customs of Britain* goes further, claiming that the pub was once haunted by this unfortunate female. Trouble started when the stone, marking the place where the supposed witch was put to death, was moved in the 1940s, to allow large army lorries easier passage. (It also notes 'scrap faggot' is an old Essex term for witch.) The barman assured me the only spirits he had seen were in the optics behind him, though he had witnessed some 'unusual happenings' in the area. Whether you believe the story or not, it is an intriguing one, especially when mulled over a pint. There were three ales available: one from Adnams (the appropriately named Ghost Ship) and two brewed exclusively for the small chain by Brentwood Brewery: namely Golden Crust with a pleasant whisky nose (ABV 3.7%) and Royal Bulldog (3.9%). The pub is mainly set out with diners in mind but I found the bar, with its self-contained seating area, welcoming for drinkers. A 2015 redecoration, and a fire about a hundred years earlier, has erased any 'olde worlde' atmosphere the place may once have had. Its aged beams, wooden floors and historical photographs and information is a pleasing combination, however. There are tales of a tunnel in the cellar linking with a nearby priory. Ambient music, outdoor seating (garden and decking).

Nearby: I found the surrounding lanes pleasant for cycling (NCN Route 16 passes nearby). The Cross Keys, White Notley, near Witham, CM8 1RQ (01376 583297) is an oak-beamed village pub with old coins nailed into a post by waggoners as advance payment for their pints. There's also a caricature mural of village inhabitants, hand painted in the 1980s.

**The Castle**, Main Road, Great Leighs, near Chelmsford, CM3 1NE. Tel. 01245 362630. www.pieandpintinns.co.uk

## GRIMLEY, WORCESTERSHIRE
### A waterside 'inn for horses'
### *Camp House*

According to the *Oxford Dictionary of English Place-names*, Grimley means 'wood haunted by a ghost or spectre'. Haunted or not, this isolated pub isn't easy to find, unless you are sailing the River Severn or walking the Severn Way. It faces the river bank, off a lane that seems to go nowhere. Dating from the fifteenth century, it occupies the site of a camp set up in 1637 by hundreds of people fleeing a plague sweeping nearby Worcester. This was as terrifying as the Great Plague of London, killing a fifth of the city's population. Those who could flee did so, others were ostracised and forced to live on Bevere Island, just to the north. They faced hunger as well as the elements, with limited help from others, as people feared contagion. In more pleasant times, the Camp House was used as a staging post for both coaches and horse-drawn barges, catering for equestrian needs as well as those of people. Stabling for a horse, donkey or mule cost 3d (1.25 pence) per night – and animals would be walked straight through the pub, as the quickest route between stables (on the site of the current kitchen) and tow-path.

The landlady told me that the pub's lantern was a landmark, akin to a lighthouse, drawing boatmen and bow-hauliers on the then busy waterway. Being so close to the water, flooding is a perennial problem. Beside a fireplace are a series of brass plaques, showing

*A summer's evening at the Camp House on the River Severn. Note the resident geese and riverside inn sign.*

the height reached by flood waters over the years. In November 2000, the bar was several feet underwater and the landlord used a punt from the front door. Seven years later, customers were boated in and out 'for the price of a pint.' The ferry was back in action during flooding in November, 2019, with potential customers being advised 'To hail ferry, toot on your car horn or phone us.'

The building resembles a small Elizabethan manor house and is much loved by the local community. How many other pubs boast an Appreciation Society on Facebook? A quarry-tiled entrance hall – complete with serving hatch – leads to a series of beamed rooms and snugs, complete with benches, settles and real fires; decorated with a jumble of darts trophies, earthenware jugs, photographs, newspaper clippings and the latest bird sightings. An expansive riverside garden, with resident families of geese, hens and peacocks, is the pub's crowning glory. There are flower beds, well-clipped lawns and a landing stage for boats. A punt ferry across the river, which had operated for centuries, ceased in the 1930s. An undercover area is useful when the boat-based Mikron Theatre Company, or other performers, arrive.

I found that sitting with a pint and watching a summertime sunset is a joy beyond compare. I almost forgot to mention the house ale: Batham's Best Bitter (ABV 4.3%). This sought-after Black Country beer is complemented by two changing guests – Thwaites Lancaster Bomber and Wainwright Golden on my last visit. Cider fans rejoice at boxes of local varieties, piled up beside the bar.

An adjacent meadow was once home home to the Camp Races, where two thousand people enjoyed horse-racing in August 1833, according to a cutting from the *Worcester Herald* displayed in the bar. A hundred years later – *circa* 1930 – hundreds of people would swim in and picnic by the Severn, when the place was known as Grimley Lido. The Wainwright family have kept the pub for decades and celebrated 80 years in June, 2019. Cash only, no cards. Meals, dog friendly, traditional games, occasional live music, camping and mooring. On CAMRA's Regional Inventory.

***Camp House Inn***, Camp Lane, near Worcester, WR2 6LX. Tel. 01905 640288.

## GUILDFORD, SURREY

### Where the Stranglers made their debut
#### *Star Inn*

When the founding members of the Stranglers, then called the Guildford Stranglers, first performed in the Star's Back Room in 1974, success undreamt of, as iconic punk rockers, lay ahead. Hundreds of other bands, solo musicians and comedians have also cut their teeth here, so it seemed ironic when I visited (March 2019) that the venue was facing being permanently silenced, due to complaints of noise by residents in a new block of flats. A campaign was mounted, including an appeal against the local authority's noise abatement ruling. The band returned to unveil a plaque marking their debut ('Stranglers back Guildford Star Inn against noise complaint that could close pub where band began', *Surrey Live*, 31 January, 2019.) More evocative were the dozens of handwritten endorsements from customers and artists pinned to beams in the bar. 'Would never have gotten where I am without the Star,' 'Spent my youth in the Star every Friday and Saturday night', 'Best memories have been made in the back room,' and so on. Thankfully, that July it was announced the brewery had won its case.

This is among the town's oldest pubs: an inn named the Star was first recorded in 1793. The Georgian building is characterful, being split into three levels, with bare floorboards, oak beams and short staircases linking the different levels. The Back Room, with its stage and bar, is entered via a narrow corridor. This dates from the 1840s, when it was called the Court Room. Long before bands performed, a branch of the Ancient Order of Forresters met there. During the twentieth century, the pub was owned by the town's Friary Brewery, later Friary Meux, which became Ind Coope in the 1960s. I found it busy with customers of varying ages. Centrally located off the High Street, it is a popular meeting place. Shepherd Neame real ales and meals are served. I enjoyed a pint of Spitfire Gold (ABV 4.1%) while trying to recall the lyrics to *No More Heroes*. My fellow customers were pleased to help. Outside seating, dog friendly, ambient music.

*Star Inn*, 2 Quarry Street, GU1 3TY. Tel. 01483 532887. www.starinnguildford.co.uk

*The plaque on the Star Inn, Guildford, was unveiled by punk band the Stranglers, which it honours. The pub is still known for its live music.*

## HASTINGS, EAST SUSSEX

### Mummified cats, smugglers and a witch
#### *Stag Inn*

The sight of two mummified cats, mounted in a glazed cabinet, greets customers entering the bar of this Grade II listed, timber-framed building. The animals were found in a first-floor chimney during renovations in the 1940s. They were entombed, according to an adjacent description, by one Hannah Clarke, who practised witchcraft in medieval Hastings. Placing cats (probably already dead) in cavities in this period was not unusual, as they were believed to protect both building and occupants against evil spirits

*Decorated here for the town's Jack-in-the-Green Festival, the Stag Inn, Hastings contains two mummified cats.*

## HAWORTH, WEST YORKSHIRE
### Haunt of the ill-fated Branwell Brontë
### *Black Bull*

and the plague, as well as scaring away vermin. The felines are not the only items discovered. In the early 1900s, a hoard of dusty Spanish doubloons and George III Spade Guineas fell from the bar ceiling, where they had been stashed during the smuggling era. Hastings was a hot-bed of this activity – smugglers would undoubtedly have frequented the inn. One of many historic buildings in the Old Town, the pub dates from the late sixteenth century – though the frontage is Georgian. It is probably the oldest in town still open.

Being a Shepherd Neame house, a selection of the Kent brewer's ales is served. As I visited during the town's annual Jack-in-the-Green Festival (early May) I was able to sample the specially brewed ale of the same name (4.2% ABV), as well as the fruity, complex Bishops Finger (5%). The pub was decorated with ribbons, while female members of staff wore floral garlands. It was busy with jovial customers attending these May Day festivities on West Hill, where the weekend climaxes with a ritual 'slaying' of a leaf-clad Jack, marking the 'release' of summer. The superstitions of Hannah Clarke's time live on. Meals, regular live music, real fires, dog friendly, garden. On CAMRA's Regional Inventory.

**Stag Inn**, 14 All Saints Street, Old Town, TN34 3BJ.
Tel. 01424 438791. www.staghastings.co.uk

Frequented by Branwell Brontë (1817-48), wayward son of the Rev. Patrick Brontë and brother of the literary siblings Charlotte, Emily and Anne, from whose pens flowed literary classics including *Jane Eyre* and *Wuthering Heights*. Here, in one of his more sober moments, Branwell was made secretary of the Freemasons' Lodge, established at the inn in 1806. It is also noteworthy for its role in railway history, as the first meetings discussing the formation of the Keighley & Worth Valley Railway – now a heritage steam line – were held within, in 1861. Perched at the top of the village's narrow, cobbled street, the Black Bull surveys not just the settlement but the brooding moors beyond.

I sat outside, on the beer terrace overlooking this atmospheric main street, with a pint of Theakston's Black Bull (ABV 3.9%). Other options were Wychwood Hobgoblin and Wainwright's Golden. Though the interior is not as rustic as the sombre stone exterior (it looks like a 1980s redecoration) the licensee was welcoming and eager to chat. She pointed out Branwell's supposed mahogany chair, set out of reach on the landing, and a copy of a letter framed on the wall. I can't vouch for the chair but the letter is fascinating. It is dated August 1853 and from the Rev. Brontë, thanking the recipient (the landlord?) for a present of a brace of game. My host hinted at unexplained phenomena – a self-smashing beer glass; and that her dog was nervous about going to the far end of the pub. (I later discovered that Haworth has become popular with paranormal societies seeking ghostly activity.) I preferred to admire the various paintings and photos, and simply relax in the same bar as that tortured artist and poet, the most misunderstood of the Brontës.

Branwell is well-known for his descent into alcoholism (gin was his drink of choice) and addiction to laudanum, though he was as creative as his sisters. In childhood, he dreamed up a fantasy

*The Black Bull, in the hilltop town of Haworth, was a drinking spot favoured by Branwell Brontë.*

## HEDGERLEY, BUCKINGHAMSHIRE
### Wassailing in the Chilterns
### *White Horse*

It has long been the custom, particularly in cider producing counties, to wassail (drink a toast to) apple trees, in order to ensure a plentiful crop next season. These high-spirited events are held near several pubs each winter, often around the second weekend of January, and the hostelries that encourage them are usually community spirited locals such as this. Buckinghamshire is not a cider county – and Hedgerley's orchard is not that long established – but such details don't stop folk who enjoy a spot of wassailing. This is an unspoilt village pub, on the edge of the Chiltern Hills, stocking a fine selection of ale and cider. Its bar counters are little more than shelves; there are no handpumps and no cellar (casks are racked in the servery, in plain view) and fires blaze in winter. The two bars are small and intimate, with extra space in a covered area at the rear.

*Beer in the White Horse, Hedgerley, is served straight from the cask. Pictured are the Datchet Border Morris Men, shortly before their January 'wassail' in the adjacent orchard.*

world, complete with role-play, that helped inspire them to write their classics. Meals, accommodation, dog friendly.

Nearby: Most visitors to the town visit the iconic Parsonage, as I did, just a few yards from the pub. There the family lived and, at age thirty-one, Branwell died. In the museum I was pleased to find a new installation: an atmospheric recreation of his candle-lit bedroom, from the 2017 BBC television drama about the family, *To Walk Invisible* (which also featured the Black Bull). As well as the unkempt bed and empty medicine bottles, there was an easel with artist's materials. Symbols of a pathetic life and unfulfilled ambition.

**Black Bull**, Haworth, Keighley, BD22 8DP. Tel. 01535 642249.
www.blackbullhaworth.com

The wassail takes place in the orchard behind the pub. A crowd of curious locals are led there, Pied Piper fashion, by the Datchet Border Morris Men playing their instruments. A bonfire is the focal point. Folk songs are sung around it while cakes (toast) are tied to the trees. I was invited to be 'butler' at the event and read the wassail 'blessing' in, I hope, a suitably rousing way, before encouraging the assembled throng to make as much noise as possible, using saucepan lids. This, apparently, is to scare away evil spirits. The wassail bowl, filled with cider, was lifted and the cry went out: 'Wassail, wassail, wassail!'

Back at the White Horse, the Morris Men and their followers order pints and promptly begin a folk music session. The ale and cider selection changes constantly. I enjoyed a Twisted Barrell mild (ABV 3.5%); six other options included Rebellion IPA (3.7%), Thirst Class Green Bullet (4.8%), Windswept APA (5%) and a selection of real ciders. Lunchtime meals, dog friendly, garden, dartboard.

*White Horse*, Village Lane, SL2 3UY. Tel. 01753 643225.
www.thewhitehorsehedgerley.co.uk

## HEMPSTEAD, ESSEX
### Birthplace of Dick Turpin
### *Bluebell Inn (formerly Rose & Crown)*

England's most notorious highwayman, who terrorized a swathe of England in the eighteenth century on his horse Black Bess, was born in this village alehouse, in 1705. His father was not only the landlord and brewer at what was then called the Bell, but also a butcher. The landlord pointed out ceiling meat-hooks in what is now a snug. He is also proud of the historical association, being knowledgeable on Turpin and displaying reproductions from 'penny dreadful' magazines of the early 1900s featuring the outlaw (*Dick Turpin: Stand and Deliver; Turpin: The Hero of Hounslow Heath*, etc.). There was also a board game, *Dick Turpin's game of Highway Robbery*.

*Notorious highwayman Dick Turpin was born in this Essex pub, which also served as his father's butcher's shop.*

Six ales were available, three of them from the local Saffron Brewery, including Session Ale (ABV 3.6%) and the delicious Agnes Waterhouse Porter (5.2%), as well as Ghost Ship and Broadside, from Adnams. The building dates from the sixteenth century, though much of that extant is from the eighteenth. The oldest part is nearest the road. There are interior oak beams, low ceilings and a wooden floor, with the focal point a large inglenook fireplace with wood-burner. There are gardens to the front and rear, with views of the parish church where Turpin was baptised. This is a pretty village and I arrived on a glorious spring evening, having driven through lovely Essex countryside, and villages such as Finchingfield. Meals are served and there is occasional live music including 'Dick Turpin jam sessions'.

Turpin was not a pleasant child:

[His] utter indifference to suffering – he once sat a woman on a fire until she told where her money was hidden – was probably instilled into him during his childhood at the Bell. Successive landlords profited from cockfights held in the arena across the lane… Acting as pot-boy for his father, young Turpin became used to cruelty while still a child.

(*The David & Charles Book of Historic English Inns.*)

There is no cruelty, just jolly banter, at the Bluebell today (I overheard one customer ask 'which actor would make a good Turpin today? That Richard O'Sullivan didn't seem right to me.') Turpin was arrested and hanged at York in 1739. The efforts of his father, still landlord at this pub, to save him were in vain. Quiet pub, dog friendly, occasional classic car meets.

***Bluebell Inn***, High Street, CB10 2PD. Tel. 01799 599199.

## HOOE, EAST SUSSEX
### A smugglers' HQ
### *Red Lion*

In April 1751, the peace of this isolated village was shattered when an armed party of Preventive Officers burst into the inn to arrest two notorious smugglers. They met with such resistance and intimidation from the assembled drinkers they were forced to retreat, fearing for their lives. We know this from a statement made by one of the Riding Officers, William Holland. Though the infamous Hawkhurst and Groombridge gangs were associated with the village, landing contraband at Pevensey Bay, this pub was headquarters of the equally unsavoury 'Hooe Company'. It was a convenient yet isolated place, 3 miles north of the coast, on the smuggling trail to Ashdown Forest. With inglenook fireplaces, candlelit tables and quarry-tiled and flagstone floors, it is suitably evocative. The licensee told me contraband was routinely hidden on the premises during the smuggling era. A bedroom cupboard has a removable panel giving secret access to storage space and the attic contains a machine once used for shredding smuggled tobacco leaves. They would be transported wrapped in hemp rope: origin of the saying 'money for old rope'.

Enjoying a nutty pint of Harvey's Sussex Bitter and a Sunday roast, I leafed through papers revealing aspects of the inn's history. Beginning as a farmhouse by 1595, a beer house licence was granted fourteen years later and, by 1805, it had become a post house, complete with livery stables and blacksmith. There are two downstairs bars and narrow stairs to an upstairs public room. Garden, real fires, dog friendly.

***Red Lion***, Hooe Common, near Battle, TN33 9EW.
Tel. 01424 892371.

*The Red Lion, Hooe was scene of unsavoury goings-on during the smuggling era.*

## KESWICK, CUMBRIA

### Home to a 'native boggart'

### *Twa Dogs Inn*

This 1960s-era pub, on the outskirts of the Lake District town, has two claims to fame. It is the only pub in England with this name, which comes from a poem by Scotland's national poet Robert Burns. He visited the town on more than one occasion. It is also home to 'the world-famous Cumbrian boggart', dating from an earlier inn on the site and displayed in the bar. A boggart is not an entity one expects to find taxidermized. Even more surprising is finding one exhibited in a pub. According to the *Oxford English Dictionary*, it is an evil or mischievous spirit.

Author Carolyne Larrington describes it as 'a native version of poltergeists...that break dishes instead of washing them, or get into the butter churn to prevent butter from forming' (pp148-9,

*A customer in the public bar plays darts, oblivious to the menacing-looking 'Cumbrian boggart' in the lounge of the Twa Dogs Inn.*

*The Land of the Green Man*, I.B. Tauris, 2017). She says they live in mounds or holes in the ground, like J.R.R. Tolkien's Hobbit, or the notorious hobthrush from North Yorkshire, and may or not be hair-covered. The one in the Twa Dogs is hairy and, to my untrained eye, resembles a cross between a badger and a fox. The bar lady could not offer much help, though she did switch on the light in its case for me. 'It's been there since the 1940s,' she sighed, 'before my time.' A notice explains that it was killed nearby in 1946; other signs offer boggart postcards for 50 pence and a polo shirt for £10. The customers seemed disinterested. A party of tourists chatted over their meals beside the blazing fire; the local darts team walked straight past and started playing in a side room festooned with rugby scarves. I sat with a pint of Jennings Bitter (there were three cask ales from this Cockermouth brewer) and found an item on the 'Museum of Hoaxes' website claiming it is an April Fool's joke from the 1980s. Members of a group called the British Boggart Preservation Society were interviewed about it on the BBC's *Nationwide* current affairs programme, it said. Meals, accommodation, garden, ambient music, occasional live music.

Nearby: The Coast to Coast cycle route and a former railway path to Threlkeld.

*Twa Dogs Inn*, Penrith Road, CA12 4JU. Tel. 017687 72599. www.twadogs.co.uk

## KINVER, STAFFORDSHIRE

### Two royal visitors – is one still there?

### *Manor House of Whittington (formerly Whittington Inn)*

This spacious hostelry has a split personality. One half is a 700-year-old, timber-framed mansion and the other a contemporary dining pub, with minimalist décor. On the summer afternoon I visited, the ancient part was deathly quiet, allowing me to roam its Grade I listed nooks and crannies in the hope of sensing its regal ghost. The

King Charles II rested briefly in 1651, during his flight from defeat at the Battle of Worcester (see page 132).

With all this history, I was hoping to see an inspired local ale or two (Burton Bridge Sovereign Gold, perhaps?) but had to content myself with a choice between Marston's Pedigree, Ringwood Boon Doggle and Wainwright Golden. This is primarily a dining pub – steaks and pizza feature prominently – but drinkers are welcome. The shiny bar, extensive patio and garden were busy. If Lady Jane Grey does still haunt, she was keeping her distance. Occasional live music, real fires.

***Manor House of Whittington***, on A449, DY7 6NY. Tel. 01384 872110. https://themanorhouseofwhittington.com

*The Manor House of Whittington has a fascinating history. It was childhood home to Lady Jane Grey, the 'nine-day queen'. Charles II also visited and it is reputedly haunted.*

ill-fated 'nine-day queen', Lady Jane Grey, lived here in childhood and reputedly returned, in haunting mode, after her execution in 1554. She is said to roam an upstairs corridor. Occasional 'ghost hunting experience nights' are held for customers in search of non-alcoholic spirits.

Built as a manor house in 1310 by Sir William Whittington – Dick Whittington's grandad – it did not become an inn for another 470 years *(David & Charles Book of Historic English Inns)*. Its clientele was unsavoury, to say the least, including murderer William Howe, arrested in 1805 while drinking in the parlour. Bull-baiting was then one of the inn's amusements. Another claim to fame is that

## LANCASTER, LANCASHIRE
### Last orders for the Pendle Witches
### *Golden Lion*

The arrest, trial and execution of the Pendle Witches is one of the saddest episodes from English history. The 1600s was an era of religious persecution and superstition. Local magistrates, keen to court favour from King James I – a monarch obsessed with witchcraft – sought to bring alleged witches to justice. A group of women (and men) living around Pendle Hill was accused by their neighbours, arrested and imprisoned in Lancaster Castle. The resulting Lancashire witch trials, held within the walls, are infamous and well documented. Ten people were found guilty. They were taken in an open cart, in a slow procession, from the castle on 20 August, 1612 and hanged together on a nearby hill – the site of Williamson Park (then moorland). The story has inspired writers and poets ever since.

On their last journey, the condemned were allowed a final drink and this is reputed to have been at this hostelry, where the ascent from the city's centre begins. A commemorative plaque, placed in 2001, lists the victims' names and that of an eleventh woman

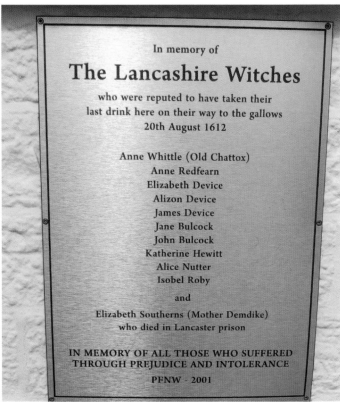

In memory of

## The Lancashire Witches

who were reputed to have taken their
last drink here on their way to the gallows
20th August 1612

Anne Whittle (Old Chattox)
Anne Redfearn
Elizabeth Device
Alizon Device
James Device
Jane Bulcock
John Bulcock
Katherine Hewitt
Alice Nutter
Isobel Roby

and

Elizabeth Southerns (Mother Demdike)
who died in Lancaster prison

IN MEMORY OF ALL THOSE WHO SUFFERED
THROUGH PREJUDICE AND INTOLERANCE

PFNW - 2001

*Lancaster's Golden Lion was last port of call for the so-called Pendle Witches shortly before their execution.*

*Plaque to the Lancashire (or Pendle) Witches on the frontage of the Golden Lion.*

who died in prison. The extant building is probably from the early 1800s and, despite its dark historical associations, I found it a cosy, welcoming pub. There are several drinking areas, including a fireside snug with armchairs and a bar with fitted benches. Six ales were on – including the delicious Pride of Pendle by Moorhouses (ABV 4.1%), one of the regular beers. The others were Castle Rock Harvest Pale, Theakston Best, Kelham Island Best, Bank Top Flat Cap and Butcombe Original; also Lilley's Sunset Cider. The pub is still sometimes called the Whittle, in deference to it once belonging to the former Whittle Springs Brewery (Anne Whittle was one of those condemned).

A gallery of local photographs decorates the walls, while a rear room is dominated by a snooker table and is used by bands and for the weekly 'open-mic' night. Outside decking, ambient music, dog friendly.

Nearby: There is a signposted Pendle Witches Trail from Pendle to Lancaster (leaflet available from local tourist offices). A tour of Lancaster Castle is recommended: it served as a prison until relatively recently.

***Golden Lion***, 33 Moor Lane, LA1 1QD. Tel. 01524 842198.
www.goldenlionpublancaster.co.uk

## LEATHERHEAD, SURREY
### The feisty alewife who inspired Henry VIII's poet
### *Running Horse*

With sloping floors and ceilings and tipsy walls, this fifteenth-century, timber-framed pub owes its fame to a saucy old poem. The *Tunning of Elenor Rumming* (aka *Elynor Rummynge*) tells the story of the eponymous Southray (Surrey) alewife who has a crooked nose and is wrinkled but brews noppy (strong) ale. Elenor's portrait graces the outside wall: she was immortalized in the words of John Skelton (*circa* 1460-1529), Henry VIII's poet laureate:

She breweth noppy ale
And maketh thereof port sale
To travellers, to tynkers,
To sweters, to swynkers,
And all good ale drynkers.

Verses from the poem are framed in the pub and can be found in full on website www.poetryfoundation.org. It runs to 135 lines, painting a jocular image of a popular brewster and her band of wretched customers, many of whom were so poor they had to barter goods for ale. Henry VIII's court was sometimes based at nearby Nonsuch Palace, when the laureate would have accompanied his fellow courtiers to fish the River Mole. The pub is a few yards from the river, so the house of Elenor Rumming was a convenient place of refreshment. According to tradition, Henry's daughter Elizabeth I slept at the inn, when the royal party was unable to cross the river in flood. With sturdy beams, an assortment of horse brasses and old prints and photos, the charming establishment is Grade II* listed. It is popular with diners. As a Shepherd Neame house, the Kent brewer's Master Brew and Spitfire were on handpull, though I enjoyed a local pint: Surrey Hills Ranmore (ABV 3.8%). Another option was Bath Ales' Prophecy (3.8%). A separate public bar offers darts and snooker; there's also a courtyard and secluded garden. Accommodation, occasional live music, dog friendly, real fire.

*The Running Horse, Leatherhead is a cosy tavern whose one-time landlady inspired a royal poet.*

*A period postcard of the Running Horse, an angler's retreat near the River Mole. Its exterior is little changed, as you can see from the accompanying photograph.*

**Running Horse**, 38 Bridge Street, KT22 8BZ.
Tel. 01372 372081. www.running-horse.co.uk

## LEIGHTON BUZZARD, BEDFORDSHIRE
### Helping disadvantaged kids
### *Black Lion*

Being awarded Pub of the Year by CAMRA's South Bedfordshire branch five years running (2015-19), and organizing regular ale and cider festivals, isn't enough for the people here. Staff (and customers) go the extra mile in their efforts helping a local charity. In the case of Paul, the bar manager when I visited, many extra miles. He told me how he'd raised £5000 cycling to Paris and then running the city's marathon. He was now planning to beat that by pedalling to Berlin, and completing the marathon there. Regular raffles and collection boxes beside the tills add £60 a month or more to the total, plus profits from a monthly pub quiz head in the same direction. It's not just about money: at Christmas, staff visit local charity Kids Out, to help wrap presents for the children. Kids Out puts fun and happiness into the lives of less fortunate children. In the words of Nikki, who runs the pub with partner Stev, 'I didn't have the greatest upbringing myself and remember benefitting from something similar as a child. This made it the perfect charity for us.'

I found eight real ales and a similar number of ciders. There's also a bottled beer menu, featuring more than a hundred mainly Belgian and German examples. Cask ales ranged from Table Beer from Cross Bay (ABV 3%) to Five Bells from Shardlow at 5%, plus brews from Nethergate, Wickwar and Oakham. The absence of screens and piped music encourages conversation – and participation in a range of club nights. These include ukulele, knitting, languages and art. Various drinking areas are set around a central servery; there are beams, wooden floors and a collection of old brewery and pub signs. There's also a piano, dartboard and beer books to browse. I stepped outside to find a courtyard garden and barn, with stillage for ale and cider festivals (it is used as a gin bar at other times). Snacks, dog friendly.

Nearby: The Leighton Buzzard Narrow Gauge Railway is a pleasant excursion for train enthusiasts, with an Ale Trail each June. The Bald Buzzard Ale House in Hockliffe Street was the town's first micro-pub.

*Black Lion*, 20 High Street, LU7 1EA. Tel. 01525 853725.
www.blacklionlb.com

*A hidden corner of the Black Lion, Leighton Buzzard. The multiple award-winning pub is known for its collection of brewery and pub signs.*

## LEINTWARDINE, HEREFORDSHIRE
### A legendary landlady
### *Sun Inn*

A blue plaque dedicated to Florence Lane, affixed to the front of this rustic stone building, proclaims: 'Flossie lived and ruled in this parlour pub.' A rare landlord to merit obituaries in *The Times* and *Daily Telegraph*, Flossie, who died, aged ninety-four in 2009, was reputed to be Britain's oldest publican. She was born in, and kept this hostelry unchanged, throughout her seventy-four-year tenure. Though new owners erected a bright, slate-floored extension at the rear in 2011, the heart of Flossie's pub remains in use. Customers still enjoy the genuine, former beer-house that was adapted from a row of cottages, *circa* 1860. It merits a place on CAMRA's National Inventory: the consumer pressure group successfully campaigned against its closure after her death.

To the left of the entrance is 'Flossie's Room', the publican's parlour, complete with family photographs, mementos, a dresser

*Legendary landlady Flossie Lane's parlour remains open to drinkers at the Sun Inn, Leintwardine.*

*Plaque outside the Sun Inn.*

and armchair, in which she held court. In her later years, customers served themselves, placing money in a jam-jar. On the right is the Redbrick Bar, named after the flooring material. Simply furnished, with long trestle tables, benches and a variety of wooden chairs, a wood-case clock above the fireplace indicates the approximate time. In her day, beer was served directly from casks in the kitchen, though there is now a bar counter in the extension, with handpumps offering four ales: Ludlow Brewing Stairway (ABV 5%) and three from Hobsons, including the wonderful Dark Nutty Mild (3.2%), and Weston's Still Cider. There is a spacious garden, laid to lawn, where I enjoyed my beer and a Welsh rarebit, one of the selection of snacks on the menu, which also included pork pies and ploughman's lunches.

On my visit, the pub was preparing to celebrate 'Flossie's Day' (her birthday) in July, with shanty singers and a hog-roast; I was also pleased that the annual tradition of electing a mock-mayor is maintained. Photographs of various strangely dressed incumbents are displayed, along with their ageing, squirrel-skin regalia. Another touching item is a framed 'Ode to Flossie Lane', penned by one of her loyal customers: '…To some she's a matriarch, to others she's the boss, but to me and my friends she's just dear old Floss…' Dog friendly, camping nearby, occasional live music.

**Sun Inn**, Rosemary Lane, SY7 0LP. Tel. 01547 540705.
www.suninnleintwardine.co.uk

## LIVERPOOL, MERSEYSIDE
### John Lennon's little-known band
### *Ye Cracke*

Hidden on a side street in the heart of the city is a time-worn boozer that could be easily missed. It is linked with a young art student named John Lennon (1940-80) and – far from being another clichéd haunt on the Beatles' tourist trail – is an atmospheric place, serving good ale. Lennon frequented it with friends while at Liverpool Art College (I was told it remains popular with students). With three others, he discussed forming a band there and they even agreed its name – the Dissenters. On at least one occasion, he took Cynthia Powell there (she would become his first wife) drinking black velvet (sparkling wine and Guinness). With its copper-topped bar counter, dark brown

*The War Office snug in Ye Cracke, Liverpool was so-called as locals discussed the progress of the Boer War there.*

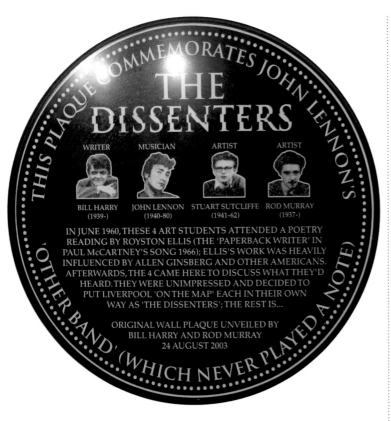

*Plaque to John Lennon's Dissenters in Ye Cracke, where the musician met with fellow art students.*

woodwork, bare floors, 1960s' fittings, veteran serving hatches and mazy electric wires, it has a faded, bohemian look. It also has a place on CAMRA's Regional Inventory. The juke-box played *Let It Be* as I sank a warming pint of Phoenix Brewery's Wobbly Bob (ABV 6%) – one of four real ales. There are period photographs showing Lennon and others outside; and a reproduction of a 1959 artwork depicting the pub, by Stuart Sutcliffe (who would later join the Beatles). The War Office is the most distinctive of the rooms, being a part-glazed snug with red leatherette banquettes. It was so named because customers discussed progress of the Boer War there (1899-1902).

A black plaque, unveiled in 2003, tells the story of the embryonic Dissenters (namely students Lennon, Sutcliffe, Bill Harry and Rod Murray) which is sometimes referred to as Lennon's 'other band'. The four had come to the pub in June 1960 after a poetry reading by Royston Ellis (the *Paperback Writer* in the eponymous Beatles' song). Unimpressed with this recital, they discussed putting Liverpool on the map in their own way. Sadly, the Dissenters never played a note. Garden.

Nearby: The Grade II* listed Philharmonic Dining Rooms, Hope Street, is one of the country's most palatial pubs (built around 1900), including the most ornate – and small – gents' toilet. A good selection of ales, too.

*Ye Cracke*, 13 Rice Street, L1 9BB. Tel. 0151 709 4171.

## LLANARMON DYFFRYN CEIRIOG, CLWYD
### The Red Hand of Chirk
### *The Hand*

A giant hand, taller than a man, is raised in silent salute outside this inn, which nestles in a beautiful Welsh valley. Why should this former drovers' retreat, now known for its fine cuisine and ale, feature such a strange statue? The pub name is not an unusual one in these parts: the Red Hand of Chirk, upon which the sculpture is based, is the symbol of the Myddleton family of Chirk Castle. It was carved by artist Jim Heath out of solid Wellingtonia (the mighty Redwood). There are bizarre legends about the symbol's origin. Lord Myddleton was on his deathbed and couldn't decide which of his twin sons should inherit the estate. So he challenged them to a horserace around the castle, the first returning to touch his bed would be the victor. One son led the race, only to fall on the staircase as they both returned. He drew his sword, sliced his hand off with one blow and threw it onto his father's bed. As this beat his brother by seconds, he claimed the inheritance. Another story says the red hand is a bloody one because it is associated with the family's misdeeds. Whether you believe these stories or not, the Hand is a perfect place to hear tales told beside a blazing log fire, its low-beamed snug bar decorated with stags' antlers. Wooden stools are lined up against the counter like ten-pins. Two ales were being served, Stonehouse Station Bitter (ABV 3.9%) and Weetwood Cheshire Cat (4%).

Beyond the bar, the stone walls of the building's construction are evident in a well-equipped games room and restaurant extension (booking advised). At about 21.45, things became eerily quiet, though not for long, according to the bar lady. 'It's the lull before the storm – we'll be full of thirsty farmers soon.' Courtyard garden, surrounded by the peaceful Ceiriog Valley. Accommodation (with spa), dog friendly.

**The Hand at Llanarmon DC**, LL20 7LD. Tel. 01691 600666.
www.thehandhotel.co.uk

*A giant hand, carved from Wellingtonia, or Redwood, outside the Hand pub in Llanarmon D.C., is evocative of a fantastic local legend.*

## LLANFIHANGEL CRUCORNEY, MONMOUTHSHIRE

### 'Wales' oldest inn' – a court and place of execution

### *Skirrid Mountain Inn*

*Reputedly haunted, the Skirrid Mountain Inn claims to be Wales' oldest inn. The house beer is Laine's Phantom Fiddler.*

Thankfully, people are no longer hanged at this inn, set at the foot of the Black Mountains. For at least five centuries things were very different, when an upstairs room housed manorial, church and assize courts. Whenever the judge handed down the death penalty, the condemned would be led from his cell on the 'mesne' floor for sentence to be carried out from the upper landing. At least 180 felons suffered this fate. A noose hangs in the stairwell, by way of gruesome emphasis. The first recorded use of the death penalty was in 1110, the defendant being one John Crowther; the last was during the Protectorate of Oliver Cromwell. Both prisoners were convicted of sheep stealing. Named after the mountain it sits below, the Skirrid (from the Welsh for shiver) claims to be the oldest in Wales. Parts of the building date back 800 years. The main bar's flagstone floor and its sturdy stone walls certainly seem ancient, as does a cavernous fireplace, with blackened pots suspended above a wood fire. The front door is medieval, as are oak beams with markings revealing their original use as ships' timbers.

There is an informative pub leaflet that claims links with Welsh Prince Owain Glyndŵr; liquid offerings to His Satanic Majesty of Devil's Brew (and its Welsh equivalent, 'Pwcca'); and the infamous 'hanging Judge', Judge Jeffreys, who held court. The house ale is Laine's Phantom Fiddler Pale (ABV 4%), named for landlord Geoff Fiddler. Other ales on offer were Wye Valley Butty Bach (4.5%) and Box Steam Skirrid Soul Train IPA (4%). As you might expect in a place so steeped in history, it is reputedly haunted. Ghost hunts, such as those run by a company called Haunted Happenings, often sell out. Meals, accommodation, ambient music, dog friendly, dartboard, garden, camping nearby.

*Skirrid Mountain Inn*, near Abergavenny (off A465), Monmouthshire NP7 8DH. Tel. 01873 890258. www.skirridmountaininn.co.uk (tribute website)

## LONDON – BARNET
### Visits from Charles Dickens and Samuel Pepys
### *Olde Mitre Inne*

I settled beside the fire on a chilly autumn day and, a pint of One Mile End's Dockers Delight in hand (ABV 4.2%), pictured illustrious customers from history coming to join me. There was Charles Dickens, said to have stayed in the 1830s and inspired to write the inn scene where the Artful Dodger educates Oliver Twist in pickpocketing. Samuel Pepys wrote about the place too, in his diaries, while lexicographer Samuel Johnson stopped by in 1774. General Monck overnighted a century before – in 1660 – on his way to restore Charles II to the throne. No wonder this rambling place of narrow corridors and aging beams oozes atmosphere.

*The stable yard of the Olde Mitre Inn, circa 1900. An alcohol licence was first granted in 1553.*

*Part of the stables of the Olde Mitre has been converted to a bar.*

The hostelry has seen a few odd events through the centuries. The strangest was in 1869, when landlord William Cobley was refused a licence for building a rat pit in the ballroom. Police discovered two dogs and 21 dead rats there, while the 'potman' was found red-handed in the fighting pit, complete with a cage containing eight live rodents. In 1787, local Justices met to discuss how to quell rioting at Barnet Fair. They reputedly drank so much that they became riotous themselves.

The Olde Mitre owes its longevity to its role as a former coaching inn on the Great North Road. Up to 150 coaches a day would pass by and many would call for a change of horses. Originally called La Roose and La Crown, there's been a pub on the site since at least 1553. The building is timber framed and Grade II listed. The extensive stables have gone, though a rear part, latterly used as a store, was converted for customer use in 2009. The archway, through which coaches entered the courtyard, now has seating. There are wood-panelled walls, stone floors, old lamps, portraits and photographs, with plenty of historical information displayed (and from which I've drawn the above highlights). Another unusual feature is the ground floor tap room, its stillage visible through a glazed door. There was an enticing ale selection, including Timothy Taylor Landlord, Tring Pale Four, Caledonian Deuchars IPA and Adnams Southwold Bitter. Meals, dog friendly, ambient music, courtyard seating.

**Old Mitre Inne**, 58 High Street, Chipping Barnet, EN5 5SJ. Tel. 0208 449 5701.

## LONDON – BELGRAVIA

### The Lord Lucan mystery
### *Plumbers Arms*

Pub-goers were startled when a distressed, blood-stained woman appeared at the bar on the night of 7 November, 1974. She said her nanny had just been murdered at her property, 46 Lower Belgrave Street, and she had been attacked by the culprit, who was still at large. Police and an ambulance were soon on the scene. Searching number 46, they found the Lucans' children unharmed but their nanny, Sandra Rivett, had been bludgeoned to death. The woman who had reported this was Lady Lucan and the

*The Plumbers Arms, where a distressed Lady Lucan ran after her children's nanny had been murdered.*

supposed murderer was Lord Lucan (he was found guilty by the jury at an inquest). His subsequent disappearance has perplexed detectives and puzzled the public ever since. Lady Lucan died in 2017, taking unanswered questions to the grave with her.

You can read the whole gruesome story in the pub, as it is neatly framed on the wall, along with another exhibit describing sightings of the wanted man. Did Lucan escape to start a new life, with a new identity, overseas or did he commit suicide by jumping from the Channel ferry? (His car was found abandoned on the Sussex coast.) We shall probably never know but one thing is for sure, this pub played a part in the night's events. The opening act in one of the most curious crime cases of modern times. Despite its upmarket location, the Plumbers, built in the 1820s, has the appearance of an ordinary corner local. On the evening of my visit, however, it had a strangely sinister look. A mirror was fringed with tangled cobwebs, spiders lurked above the bar and what appeared to be a human skeleton was hanging from a cast-iron column. No, I hadn't stumbled upon Lord Lucan's mortal remains: this was October and they were merely Halloween decorations. I sat with a pint of Harvey's Sussex Bitter – other options were Robinson's Unicorn, and Abbott and IPA from Greene King – and contemplated the mystery. Other customers, including parties of tourists from the USA and Holland, seemed more interested in planning their night 'on the town'. The ground floor bar is small and, upstairs, is a cosy and even smaller room. There's a rare accessory, once common in pubs: a working bell-push, used to summon staff. Meals, ambient music, dog friendly, closed Sunday.

*Plumbers Arms*, 14 Lower Belgrave Street, SW1W 0LN. Tel. 0207 730 4067. www.greeneking-pubs.co.uk

## LONDON – BETHNAL GREEN
### Once owned by the Kray Twins
### *Carpenters Arms*

Bethnal Green was the 'manor' of the notorious 1960s' gangsters, Reggie and Ronnie Kray. Apart from its food menu and some clear windows, this street corner local and former Truman's tied house has changed relatively little since they lived a hundred yards away. The pub has more than a passing link to the twins, as they bought it in 1967 as a gift to their mother, Violet. 'It was where Reggie Kray had a drink on 29 October, 1967, to settle his nerves before going to murder Jack McVitie. The Krays liked the pub because it was narrow and had just one entrance, which meant they could see anyone coming in.' (*Caterer Licensee Hotelier*, 8 January, 2019). The magazine observes they attended Wood Close School, situated behind the pub, while their old boxing club is midway between the hostelry and their former home.

The Carpenters boasts bare boards, panelled walls and a simple fireplace. The evil twins' eyes, depicted on a cartoon-like portrait beside a pair of sash windows, seem to follow customers returning to their benches with drinks. A narrow corridor, lit by 1930s-era lights, links a rear room that is quite hidden away, so would be convenient for planning a bank heist. Visiting at dusk, I found table candles lit and lights dimmed: niceties that would have been alien to the Krays. Situated close to trendy Brick Lane, these days the Carpenters attracts young people coming for gastronomy and gin, as well as ale lovers. Real ales were Timothy Taylor Landlord and Adnams Mosaic. Patio garden, dog friendly, ambient music.

*Carpenters Arms*, 73 Cheshire Street, E2 6EG. Tel. 0207 739 6342.   www.carpentersarmsfreehouse.com

*Parts of the Carpenters Arms still resemble the back-street boozer it was when the Kray twins bought it. They reportedly liked it because it only had one entrance!*

## LONDON – BISHOPSGATE

### Nathaniel Bentley's bizarre relics
### *Dirty Dick's*

The saying 'fact is stranger than fiction' was never truer than when applied to the origin of this popular pub's name. It was the nickname of Nathaniel Bentley, a wealthy eighteenth-century merchant and dandy, who lived in nearby Leadenhall Street. Nathaniel was betrothed to an attractive, well-connected lady who fell ill and died on the day of their marriage. He promptly locked up the room where their wedding breakfast was laid out and sank into despair. He failed to wash, lived in squalor and didn't even bury his cats when they died. His cobweb-encrusted wedding breakfast may have inspired Charles Dickens' Miss Havisham in *Great Expectations*. On Nathaniel's retirement in 1804 the landlord of a nearby pub (then variously named the Old Port Wine House and Old Jerusalem) bought the decaying warehouse relics to decorate his establishment, which he renamed Dirty Dick's. When

*Dirty Dick's inn sign includes an artist's impression of an eighteenth-century landlord whose nickname it carries: the eccentric Nathaniel Bentley.*

*Some of Nathaniel Bentley's artefacts on display in Dirty Dick's, Bishopsgate.*

that was demolished, *circa* 1870, the exhibits were saved for a new one on the site, now part of the Young's chain. Whereas the items used to fill the entire pub, in 1985 most were taken away, with the remainder relegated to a glazed cabinet at the rear. So do squeeze your way through the crowd to admire mummified cats, a petrified fish, rusting kettle and other bizarre ornaments. Be warned though, they may put you off your dinner.

Ales are from the Young's range, plus guests: I enjoyed a St Austell Proper Job. Meals served, upstairs restaurant. A basement bar serves craft beers and cocktails. Nearby: Opposite are Liverpool Street station and the ornate Hamilton Hall pub, featured in my book *Unusual Railway Pubs, Refreshment Rooms & Ale Trains* (Halsgrove, 2013 and 2018).

**Dirty Dick's**, 202-204 Bishopsgate, Liverpool Street, EC2M 4NR. Tel. 0207 283 5888. www.dirtydicks.co.uk

## LONDON – BLOOMSBURY
### Clock recalls a wartime tragedy
### *Dolphin Tavern*

The hands of a battered wall clock are set forever at 10.40pm, the time when a bomb from a German airship fell from the sky, badly damaging this corner pub. The timepiece was recovered from the rubble. I wonder whether they had any warning – in World War I, attack from the air was a totally new form of aggression. Three men died that fateful night – 8 September, 1915 – after the cargo of high explosive had been released from a German Army Zeppelin drifting silently, eight thousand feet above the capital. It was among the first raids of this sort and one of the deaths was of a fireman who attended the scene. One of the airship captains wrote in his log: 'The explosive effect of the 300kg bomb must be very great, since a whole row of lights vanished in one stroke.' The Zeppelin's crew of 17 must have been too frozen to cheer, wrapped up as they were in layers of clothes against the temperature, minus 30°C.

The single-room pub is decorated with many items of paraphernalia, though none are as poignant as this rusty timepiece. The clock is surrounded by some period photographs and a copy of the census of 1911. This shows members of the Barnes family and a young female servant were in residence. It was rebuilt after the war but has a retro feel to it. On a rainy Friday evening, I found it busy with a lively after-work crowd. The barman was chatty after my request to photograph the timepiece. He told me about a nameless bar in France, the 'first to be liberated in WWII', that charges ten Euros a pint and allows no-one to take photos. 'You have to buy their own postcards' he said. 'Many people take photos here without restriction. Perhaps we should install a British Legion charity box.'

I enjoyed a pint of Timothy Taylor's Landlord (ABV 4.3%); other options were Adnams Ghost Ship and St Austell Tribute. Meals, quiet pub, outdoor area.

*This old clock in the Dolphin Tavern is forever set at 10.40pm, the time the pub was damaged by a bomb dropped from a Zeppelin airship.*

**Dolphin Tavern**, 44 Red Lion Street, WC1R 4PF. Tel. 0207 831 6298.

## LONDON – BOROUGH
### A remarkable inn with many stories
### *George Inn*

There aren't many pubs that have a 350-page paperback devoted to them, but the Grade I listed George is no ordinary boozer. *Shakespeare's Local* by Pete Brown (Macmillan, 2012) tells the story of London's last remaining galleried coaching inn. An inn has stood here, off Borough High Street, since at least 1542, making it the lone survivor, says Brown, on a street that once boasted the highest concentration of inns in the United Kingdom. The location was strategic: close to London Bridge, for centuries the only road entry point to the city from south of the River Thames and the starting point for stage coaches. The George stood next to the famous Tabard, which was immortalized by Chaucer as place of departure for his storytelling pilgrims, in *The Canterbury*

*The George Inn, occupying a yard off Borough High Street, was known to William Shakespeare and Charles Dickens. It is London's last galleried inn. Storytelling is underway in the Parliament Bar, nearest the camera.*

*Tales.* The current incarnation of the George dates from a 1676 rebuilding, after the great fire of Southwark. It is now in the care of the National Trust and leased to brewer Greene King. As well as the Suffolk brewery's ales, including IPA and Abbott, and the house staple, George Inn Ale (ABV 4%), I found two brews from farther afield, namely Timothy Taylor's Landlord (4.3%) and Cranberry Sauce Stout (5.2%) from Portobello.

Charles Dickens mentions the establishment in *Little Dorrit*; William Shakespeare knew it as well and refers to it in his play *King John*. Both writers would be surprised that only one wing remains, the two others being demolished by the Great Northern Railway for warehousing, when coaching inns declined in popularity. The remaining building, which faces a courtyard, is cavernous – a maze of rooms, with dark wooden floors and sombre wall panelling. Creaking stairs climb to the former bedrooms, stacked like the decks of an ageing galleon. In the oldest surviving part, nearest the road, is the Parliament Bar, its fireplace housing a stove. Secured to the far wall is perhaps the inn's most important curio: its Act of Parliament Clock. Made around 1750, it is named after a tax on watches and clocks imposed in 1797 by William Pitt the Younger. To quote Pete Brown:

> …the day was saved by wily publicans and their famous 'tavern clocks'. Saintly publicans selflessly installed these clocks…so that people could pop in at frequent intervals to check what time it was. If they divined that the time was beer o'clock – well surely that was Pitt's fault too, wasn't it?

As the clock was installed almost fifty years before the said act, perhaps it is something of a misnomer. Pitt eventually repealed the unpopular tax on time and replaced it with… the first permanent income tax. Outdoor seating in courtyard, meals served.

***George Inn***, 77 Borough High Street, SE1 1NH.
Tel. 020 7407 2056. www.greeneking-pubs.co.uk

## TWELFTH NIGHT FESTIVAL

A jolly procession, led by a weird and wonderful band of characters, streams into the George Inn's courtyard early in January. They are there to celebrate Twelfth Night in a colourful and joyous manner: one that audiences from Shakespeare's time would recognise. Lead character of this throng is the Holly Man, dressed from head to toe in holly and ivy, the winter guise of the Green Man from pagan myths (and pub signs). Father Christmas, King George, a Turkish Knight, a Doctor and Beelzebub (the Devil) are fellow performers in this motley troop, who arrive thirsty after performing a Mummers' Play beside Shakespeare's Globe Theatre on the South Bank. They mingle with the crowd as musicians, also in costume, strike up accordion, fiddle and drum. Two members of the public, who have been declared King Bean and Queen Pea for the day, are serenaded. Folk dancers twirl and whirl in front of the inn's historic galleries. There is storytelling in the Parliament Bar, the singing of carols, and mulled wine is served. Outside, customers are encouraged to join in the singing and tie a ribbon on the Kissing Wishing tree.

I found it an enjoyable way to end the Christmas holiday period, in an otherwise drab month. The George's courtyard setting, as dusk falls, is magical. The free event has been staged annually for twenty-five years, by a group of actors and musicians under the patronage of Sir Mark Rylance. Called 'the Lions part' (www.thelionspart.co.uk), its fusion of street performance, music and storytelling has origins in the midwinter plays that were performed throughout Europe from the fourteenth century.

*The Holly Man, winter incarnation of the medieval Green Man, laughs with a twenty-first century customer during the George Inn's Twelfth Night Festival.*

## LONDON – BOW

### A grieving mother began an Easter tradition
### *Widow's Son*

This East End corner pub comes to life each Good Friday, when a party of Royal Navy sailors (from HMS *President* when I visited) arrive with a fresh hot cross bun. One of the ratings is hoisted on the others' shoulders and, to applause from the assembled throng, places it in a net full of older buns that hang from the ceiling. Fresh ones are distributed among the crowd and the merriment continues for hours. One of the strangest customs in the capital, its origin (and that of the pub's name) comes from the story of a widow who lived here and baked a bun at her son's request.

Serving on his first Navy voyage in the 1780s, he told her he'd be home at Easter. He did not return and was later reported lost at sea. His body was never found. The sailor's mother baked a new bun each year and hung them up one by one, in the vain hope that he would return someday. When she died and the cottage was replaced by a tavern (*circa* 1848) the tradition was continued by the landlord and his successors.

Though redecorated in recent years, the Grade II* listed Victorian building retains fittings from the 1870s, including engraved mirrors and decorative panels. Expect a sailor or two among the customers at any time of year. No real ale, food served, garden, occasional live music.

*A naval rating from HMS* President *drops to the floor after placing a hot cross bun into the basket at the Widow's Son, in 2015. The ceremony is held each Good Friday.*

***Widow's Son***, 75 Devons Road, E3 3PJ. Tel. 0203 069 7426. http://widowsson.co.uk

## LONDON – CAMDEN TOWN

### A deadly duel
### *Colonel Fawcett (formerly Camden Arms)*

One of the last fatal duels fought in Britain took place on the Camden Road, in 1843. The mortally wounded combatant, thirty-four-year-old Col. Fawcett of the 55th Regiment of Foot, was brought to this public house – then and until recent years called the Camden Arms – to be nursed through his last hours. Aside from the pub's current name, the only reminder I found is two framed exhibits adjacent to the ladies' loo. One of these is an extract from a book, *Old and New London, Vol. 5, The Northern Suburbs: Holloway*, published in 1878. It states that the duel, carried out between the colonel and one Lt. Munro – they were brothers-in-law as well as brothers-in-arms – took place in grounds of another tavern, the Brecknock Arms. It records that the challenge, early on a Saturday morning, was caused by a 'hasty expression regarding some family differences' (apparently, the slight included an insult to Fawcett's wife). It led to the colonel, suffering a dangerous chest gunshot wound, being assisted to the Brecknock. He was denied admission '…so he was taken to the Camden Arms, where he died the following Monday.'

These days, Camden is usually a calmer place, despite the tourist throngs, and the pub is popular with diners. I settled for a pint of Tiny Rebel's Hank (ABV 4%), a hoppy, golden ale, though I could have chosen that brewer's Chewy Stout (5.6%) or the local Hammerton N1 Pale (4.1%). There is an impressive gin menu, with about a hundred offered, according to the barman. He added that the gin specialism is linked to stories about the late colonel, who quaffed this spirit while entertaining visitors during his final hours. The bare-boards pub has a rustic charm, enhanced by distressed wooden furniture and slate fire surrounds. The bar counter occupies a compact corner, there is roadside seating and a rear patio garden, with its own bar. There is another bar upstairs, used for regular events. A former high-level railway, which may eventually become the capital's version of New York's popular

*Artist's impression of a gun duel between nineteenth-century gentlemen. The Colonel Fawcett pub name commemorates the loser of a duel who was carried there to spend his final hours.*

'High Line' pedestrian walkway, is behind the pub.

There is a postscript to the above story. A series of trials followed, since the activity of duelling and assisting with it were, and remain, serious offences:

The inquest found the duellist had been murdered by his opponent; the seconds and attending doctor were charged with murder in the second degree. Yet after a series of trials, only the duellist was convicted, with the jury giving a strong recommendation for mercy. …The judge, even as he passed the death sentence, assured the prisoner it would not be carried out. (Judith Flanders, *The Victorian City, Everyday Life in Dickens' London*, Atlantic Books, 2012.)

**Colonel Fawcett**, 1 Randolph Street, NW1 0SS. Tel. 0207 267 9829. http://thecolonelfawcett.co.uk

## LONDON – CUDHAM
### Big boots for a little comedian
### *Blacksmith's Arms*

Situated on the wooded fringes of Greater London, close to the Kent border, this was birthplace of one of the greatest music hall comedians. According to exhibits in the pub, 'Little Tich' (real name Harry Relph, 1867-1928) was one of 15 children born to landlord Richard Relph. Though only 4ft 6in (137cm) tall, he became a celebrity on both sides of the Atlantic. His most famous act was the Big Boot Dance, performed wearing boots with extended soles, enabling him to lean over at impossible angles. The extraordinary footwear is on display and there is an illustration of him in action; also a blue plaque. Relph developed his acting skills at any early age by mimicking entertainers employed in his father's pub, going on to perform in other Kentish hostelries before becoming smitten

*The Blacksmith's Arms was birthplace of a music-hall comedian – one of fifteen children born to landlord Richard Relph.*

*Just walk in these shoes: An example of Little Tich's trademark footwear is displayed, alongside a plaque honouring him, in the bar of the Blacksmith's Arms.*

by the music hall. Pantomime appearances with the likes of Dan Leno and Marie Lloyd followed. He was also remarkable for having a partly webbed extra digit on each hand.

The Blacksmith's Arms began as a farm dwelling, *circa* 1628, becoming home to a blacksmith and beer retailer who got his first licence in 1729. Its hilltop location boasts bucolic views, while the interior has an Edwardian feel, with wooden beams, dado and picture rails. The menu attracts diners from a wide area but drinkers are also welcome. I enjoyed a pint of Harvey's Best, other options being Sharp's Doom Bar and Greene King IPA. There is a large garden full of colour in summer; surrounding paths and lanes are a delight for walkers and cyclists. Charles Darwin's home, Down House, is another nearby attraction. Dog friendly, real fire.

***Blacksmith's Arms***, Cudham Lane South, near Sevenoaks, TN14 7QB. Tel. 01959 572678. www. theblacksmithsarmscudham.com

## LONDON – DEPTFORD

### Jack in the Green's revival
### *Dog and Bell*

It was in Thames-side Deptford that, in 1593, history's most infamous tavern murder took place: that of the Elizabethan playwright Christopher Marlowe. The twenty-nine-year-old, whose works influenced William Shakespeare, is said to have died after a drunken beer-house quarrel, following a day's smoking and playing backgammon. The said house no longer exists but, just off the High Street is this popular hostelry. It is a rarity in modern London: a back-street community local with an excellent range of beer and cider. It is also the place where an 8-foot-tall gentleman, dressed entirely in leaves and flowers, begins his annual outing each May Day. Re-started in the 1980s, the Deptford Jack-in-the-Green Parade (www.deptford-jack.org.uk) is the revival of a nineteenth-century tradition. One of many 'start of spring' traditions seen in

folklore, in this one chimney-sweeps paraded 'Jack' around various towns, collecting money to buy provisions over the summer, when there were few chimneys to clean.

The pub has polished wood tables, benches and chairs. An array of maritime-themed artworks and brewery mirrors adorn the walls. Above the curving bar counter are garlands of dried hops, while six hand-pulls are serving tempting ales, including Great Heck Trafalgar (ABV 4%) and Mount Hood (4.5%) and Hammerton Pentonville Oyster Stout (5.3%). Biddenden is one of six scrumpy ciders, while a blackboard displays an impressive selection of mainly Belgian bottled beers. There is an array of board games and a shove-ha'penny board awaiting their next turn of duty. An antique bar billiards table has pride of place. On my 1 May visit, it was open and busy by 11am, with everyone (participants and public) chatting and drinking in anticipation of the day ahead. As well as Jack in all his verdant finery, there is the rest of Fowlers Troop – its members in Edwardian or fancy dress, with elaborate green-themed clothes, sprigs of ivy and laurel, and make-up. Most of the preparations were completed the previous evening.

*Accompanied by musicians and colourful banners, an eight-foot high human tree, known as Jack-in-the-Green, begins his march from the Dog and Bell. The tradition was begun locally by chimney sweeps in the nineteenth century.*

Shortly before midday, everyone assembles outside and the sound of accordions, hurdy-gurdies and drums fill the air. Jack has his floral costume placed over him and the procession sets off on a musical march through the streets of Deptford, along the river and around Greenwich. Children wave in excitement, locals and tourists smile, snapping away with their phones. The parade makes extended calls at several other pubs, until the whole ensemble collapses, exhausted but happy, into the Ashburnham Arms (page 80) at the end of the afternoon. It was satisfying to see the Dog and Bell in carnival mood but I would happily return any other day. Regular beer festivals are held – and a competitive Pickle Festival in November. Meals, patio at rear, dog friendly, ambient music.

**Dog and Bell**, 116 Prince Street, Deptford, SE8 3JD. Tel. 0208 692 5664.

## LONDON – DOCKLANDS
### Nerve-centre of the world's largest dock
*Ledger Building*

London was once the world's greatest port and this was the headquarters of West India Docks, opened in 1802 as the most important one in the capital. Though the sailing ships and their cargoes of rum, sugar and spices are long departed, the setting remains impressive. It occupies a cobbled quayside, surrounded by the towering office blocks of Canary Wharf and lofty cranes. The Ledger Building was 'mission control': West India was the world's largest dock of its type, able to handle six hundred ships. I entered through the original Greek Doric portico, into a stately hall, with a bar situated in the former main office. Remarkably little changed, the building once also housed a police office, dock superintendent's office, a boardroom and strong room. This had a reinforced 'Reliance' door (added in 1889, now hidden behind the bar). In these offices, dozens of ledger clerks once beavered away. The offices were originally unheated, to avoid the risk of chimney sparks falling on highly inflammable warehouses. This made

*The Ledger Building, opened in 1802, housed the headquarters of one of the world's most important docks. Rows of clerks beavered away at desks where the bar is now situated.*

them bitterly cold in winter, until 1829, when staff persuaded the company to install a hot-air heating system. This not only proved unreliable but highly dangerous, due to noxious fumes and an unreliable pumping engine. The system was replaced by water-based central heating in 1848. The offices were subsequently enlarged, to cope with the growing work of the dock, with clerks installed behind long rows of desks.

Sitting in the large and busy bar, with its lantern roof, truss supports and rounded Georgian windows, I imagined customers as clerks of old, holding quill pens instead of drinks, inking the latest consignments on dog-eared ledgers. The pub is part of the J.D. Wetherspoon chain, so has their wide range of real ales and food served all day. I enjoyed a Powder Monkey (ABV 4.4%) from Nelson Brewery; an appropriate choice, as it is brewed at another historic dockyard, Chatham in Kent. Don't miss the West India Dock foundation plaque of 1800, which occupies almost a whole exterior wall. Outside seating, adjacent to dockside.

Nearby: The Museum of London Docklands is next-door, occupying another old warehouse.

**Ledger Building**, 4 Hertsmere Road, West India Quay, E14 4AL. Tel. 0207 536 7770. www.jdwetherspoon.com

## LONDON – EARLS COURT
### Bob Dylan's first London performance
### *Troubadour*

Entrance is through a curious black door, carved with effigies of angels, humans and the devil, all playing musical instruments. Inside, this theme continues, with dozens of time-worn instruments hanging from ceiling and walls. An enamel sign announces 'Organs and Street Cries Prohibited'. There are bare floorboards, mirrors advertising ales and vintage signs. There's a jumble of tables and chairs and, behind a battered wooden counter, a barista polishes glasses. Since its opening in 1954, the Troubadour has been a bohemian West London meeting place, a licensed coffee bar rather than a pub, notable for its roll-call of celebrities (performers and customers). There is no real ale: keg beers are from Meantime and there is a small but well-chosen range of bottled beers and ciders. I settled for a warming Meantime Chocolate Porter (ABV 6.5%), while my friend had a Weihenstephan Weissbier (5.4%).

This was where Bob Dylan first performed in the capital. Paul Simon, Charlie Watts, Sammy Davis Jr., Jimi Hendrix, Tom Robinson and Elvis Costello all followed in his footsteps. Actor Richard Harris fell in love with his wife Elizabeth here (she was doing the washing up). Director Ken Russell recruited staff for his first shorts and became friends with Oliver Reed. Early copies of

*Star bar: the Troubadour is decorated with a variety of ephemera. Paul Simon, Jimi Hendrix and Bob Dylan are among those who performed there.*

satirical magazine *Private Eye* were conceived at its tables and the anti-nuclear 'Ban the Bomb' meetings were held (this information is from the establishment's website). Though it has expanded into former shops on either side, the Troubadour survives as a hybrid of 1950s-era meeting place and continental-style café. Décor includes LP record sleeves featuring period photographs. Live music is staged in the basement. There's a unisex toilet. Meals, ambient music, courtyard.

*Troubadour*, 263-267 Old Brompton Road, London SW5 9JA. Tel. 020 7341 6333. www.troubadourlondon.com

## LONDON – FARRINGDON
### Pawnbrokers to a gambling monarch
### *The Castle*

Few people notice three gold balls – the age-old pawnbrokers' symbol – displayed outside this lofty pub. The Castle is, reputedly, Britain's only hostelry to hold a pawnbroker's licence. Though situated opposite an important railway hub, Farringdon, it had its 'fifteen minutes of fame' (to mis-quote Andy Warhol) before

*Three spheres, traditional symbol of a pawnbroker, are displayed at first floor level, on the Castle in Farringdon.*

any tracks were laid. It was granted special permission by King George IV (who reigned from 1820-30). The monarch borrowed cash from the landlord after gambling away his ready money at a cockfight in Clerkenwell. The area, then known as Hockley-in-the-Hole, was rough and had many cock-fighting rings. The king did not reveal his identity but left a pocket watch and chain as security. A royal messenger came to redeem it the following day.

The tavern keeper later received a Royal Warrant, entitling him to advance money on pledges in perpetuity. A pawnbroker's licence was then issued, though it has not been used, certainly not in recent times. A large painting is displayed in the downstairs bar, showing the king dressed as a gentleman, proffering his timepiece to the landlord. Beneath is a wooden plaque describing the story, drawn from records held at Finsbury public library. Real ales from Timothy Taylor, St Austell and Sharp's on my visit. Meals (upstairs dining room), ambient music.

*The Castle*, 34 Cowcross Street, London EC1M 6DB. Tel. 0207 253 2892. www.thecastlefarringdon.co.uk

## LONDON – GREENWICH
### Getting a lift from the Morris Men
### *The Gipsy Moth and Ashburnham Arms*

Easter Monday can be spent in an uplifting way if you visit the Thames-side town of Greenwich. The Blackheath Morris Men have revived a custom that was once held in many parts of England but has otherwise died out. Passers-by and tourists stared in disbelief as the troop interrupted their folk dancing every few minutes to encourage a female into a chair garlanded with spring flowers. Once seated, she was lifted high in the air three times, as the chair was turned. There seemed no shortage of volunteers for this bizarre ritual. In the space of fifteen minutes, I watched Melanie from Hamburg, Karen from Bromley and Freya from Norway undergo the lift and spin, with big grins on their faces.

*A member of the public is lifted and twirled on a flower-garlanded chair by the Blackheath Morris Men in Greenwich. It is the continuation of the Easter Lifting tradition, possibly once part of fertility rites.*

Pubs are central to this event, not only because Morris Men are thirsty but they also provide a ready-made audience.

The lifting takes place at several locations around town over a five-hour period, but they are either outside or close to the Gipsy Moth for much of the time. This pub's location is dramatic, in the shadow of the preserved tea-clipper *Cutty Sark*. It is spacious, extends to a conservatory and patio and serves craft beers, meals and had two ales on hand-pull.

After the main event, I adjourned to the Ashburnham Arms with the Morris Men for an informal 'folkie' jam session, though the floral chair had been abandoned by then. The 'Ash', as it's known, is an unspoilt back-street local in a conservation area of stuccoed terraces. It's the troop's base on Thursday evenings, after practice at a nearby hall. A tied house belonging to Kent brewer Shepherd Neame – I found their Master Brew Bitter and Whitstable Bay on hand-pump – it is a multi-room hostelry with bare floorboards, a sturdy wooden bar, patio garden and no piped music. The rear room, where the musicians gather, is named Pamela's Lounge after the pub's cat. One of the dancers told me he remembered the pub

in the 1970s when it was busy with students. 'There was no food then, it was very basic with a strict landlady who wouldn't stand for any rowdy behaviour.' Even so, the landlord, her husband, ran a gambling corner, playing cards for serious money.

The origins of the tradition of Easter Lifting (or Heaving) are obscure. It is probably a remnant of an older agricultural custom, perhaps a rite of fertility, to foster the growth of healthy crops. The event was often an excuse for rowdiness and frowned upon by the Church. *(Dictionary of British Folk Customs.)*

Nearby: Number 7 Ashburnham Grove bears a plaque stating that the writer Edgar Wallace was born there (1875). Best known today for scripting the film *King Kong*, he wouldn't have known the Ashburnham Arms, as his destitute mother sent him to foster parents at nine days old.

**Gipsy Moth**, 60 Greenwich Church Street, SE10 9BL. Tel. 0208 858 0786. www.thegipsymothgreenwich.co.uk
**Ashburnham Arms**, 25 Ashburnham Grove, SE10 8UH. Tel. 0208 355 5141. www.ashburnham-arms.co.uk

## LONDON – HAMPSTEAD
### Famous authors – and an infamous highwayman
### *Spaniards Inn*

Of numerous pubs claiming association with highwayman Dick Turpin, none is more renowned than this one. Set on the edge of Hampstead Heath, high above London, it began as a tollgate inn, around 1585. The present, part timber-framed and weather-boarded building dates from the following century. After preying on coach travellers crossing the heath, Turpin is said to have hidden in the cellars, though the claim he was born here is false (see Bluebell, page 56). It has several other claims to fame, however, featuring in the pages of Bram Stoker's *Dracula* and Charles Dickens' *The Pickwick Papers*. Lord Byron and John Keats also supped here and, during the Gordon Riots of 1780, a mob

*Spaniards Inn, on the edge of Hampstead Heath, contains a labyrinth of old rooms, including the atmospheric Turpin Bar, upstairs.*

paused *en route* to attacking Kenwood House. They were stopped by the landlord, who kept them talking (and probably drinking) until soldiers arrived to arrest them. The house survived, is open to the public and is a few minutes' walk away.

Spaniards is an atmospheric place, particularly on quiet winter evenings. The interior is a jumble of rooms, with low ceilings and wood-panelled walls, with high-back settles and time-worn furniture. Upstairs is the wonderful, panelled Turpin Bar, with its creaking wooden floor. There were four real ales on my visit: Hop Back Summer Lightning (ABV 5%) and the hoppy Adnams Mosaic (4.1%), as well as Sharp's Doom Bar and Fuller's London Pride. On a sunny afternoon, the wooded beer garden is popular: you'll need to arrive early to claim a table at Sunday lunchtimes. It benefits from all the ambience of a country inn, though is less than 4 miles from central London. On CAMRA's Regional Inventory. Meals, dog friendly.

**Spaniards Inn**, Spaniards Road, NW3 7JJ. Tel. 0208 731 8406.
www.thespaniardshampstead.co.uk

## LONDON – HIGHBURY
### Pleasure gardens – and riots
### *Highbury Barn*

The Highbury Barn was a renowned entertainment venue in the nineteenth century. Its expansive grounds – close to the eponymous pub – began as a genteel, rural retreat but became, like Vauxhall Pleasure Gardens, an often rowdy place with 'vulgar attractions'. Catering for thousands, with a vast dancing platform, hot-air balloon rides, high-wire acts, pantomime and music hall, it attracted disreputable characters, including prostitutes. With the increasingly bawdy behaviour of its patrons, climaxing in a near riot by students from St Bartholomew's Hospital, it was forced to close down in 1871.

*Highbury Barn stands near the site of the notorious Victorian pleasure gardens of the same name. A green plaque commemorates the Peasants' Revolt of 1381.*

A plaque on the pub wall records an earlier and much more calamitous riot. This was part of the Peasants' Revolt (against the Poll Tax) in 1381. A furious mob of 20,000 people marched on Highbury Manor House, which once stood adjacent. Then the home of the Grand Prior of the Knights Hospitaller, who enforced the tax, the crowd made it a target and razed it to the ground. All that remained was the above Barn.

Today, the area is much more restrained, though the pub can get lively on Arsenal FC match days. A busy community venue, it boasts outdoor seating on a tree-lined piazza, overlooking a lofty ceremonial archway. When I visited, it was taking part in a 'N5 Ale Crawl', showcasing 25 breweries from London, in collaboration with three other pubs. A large, wood-floored bar is decorated in contemporary style. It was buzzing with (mainly young) customers. Family groups were dining in an adjoining restaurant. Meals, dog friendly, regular live music.

*Highbury Barn*, 26 Highbury Park, N5 2AB.
Tel. 0207 226 2383. www.thehighburybarn.com

## LONDON – ISLINGTON (1)

### A music-hall song

### *Eagle*

*The Eagle occupies the site of a well-known music-hall that was the subject of a famous song. Singer Marie Lloyd made her first appearance there, in 1885.*

*Up and down the City Road*
*In and out the Eagle*
*That's the way the money goes*
*Pop goes the weasel*

A golden eagle looks down from its rooftop cupola perch, surveying this grandiose pub just off City Road. Part of the popular song that immortalizes it adorns one wall. It occupies the site of one of the capital's most colourful music-hall pubs, the Eagle Tavern (formerly Shepherd and Shepherdess). A weasel was a tool used in leatherwork by saddlers, one of whom lived on nearby Nile Street and 'popped' (or pawned) it to obtain his admission money. Entrance was eightpence (less than four pence today) which included 'sixpenny-worth of grog'. For the price, customers were entertained by popular singers and, when a pleasure garden opened on the site, there were circus acts and hot-air balloon launches. In 1824, one of these stunts ended in disaster when an aeronaut named Harris died, crashing in distant Carshalton. A thirteen-year-old, named Miss Stocks, whom he took along for the ride, survived and went on to become a minor celebrity. Plunging balloons aside, the Eagle was so successful that a gaslit concert

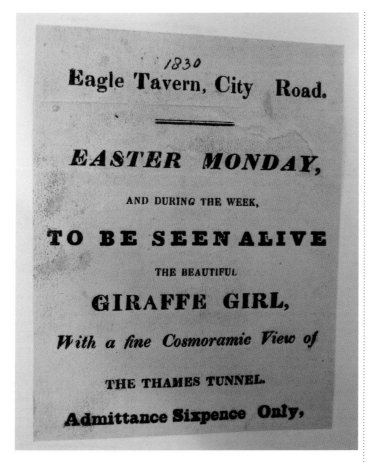

*A handbill, dated 1830, gives a hint as to the sort of entertainment once enjoyed at the Eagle.*

wall tiling and a parquet floor, the place has a somewhat faded grandeur. The main reminder of past glories is a plaque by the Borough of Hackney confirming the tavern and pleasure grounds stood here (1825-1899) and the famous music-hall singer Marie Lloyd made her first public performance on its stage (1885). Meals served, courtyard seating. Nearby: The Wenlock Arms, 26 Wenlock Road, N1 7TA, a back-street real ale gem beloved of CAMRA members.

*Eagle*, 2 Shepherdess Walk, N1 7LB. Tel. 0207 250 0507.
www.theeaglehoxton.co.uk

## ISLINGTON (2)

### Film studios where Alfred Hitchcock cut his teeth
### *North by Northwest (formerly North Pole)*

I don't know if legendary film director Alfred Hitchcock was a pub goer, though he was partial to White Lady gin. This corner pub was reputedly extant at the time he began his career at nearby studios. The studio site, now apartments, is a couple of minutes' walk away: a brown plaque names it as Gainsborough Film Studios (1924-49) – though it actually began as Islington Studios five years before. Actors and studio technicians would have called into the pub during breaks in filming. Since 2014, it has capitalized on the link by becoming a 'theme pub' that delights film fans. I supped a pint of the floral (and local) Hammerton N1 (ABV 4.1%) as models of crop-duster biplanes from the titular Hitchcock movie appeared to sweep down from the ceiling. I counted five such aircraft, recalling the nerve-wracking farmland scene where Cary Grant tries to outrun the killer 'plane.

Portraits of Hitchcock gaze at customers from every angle, and there are colourful posters of his most memorable movies. *The Man Who Knew Too Much*, *Psycho*, *The 39 Steps*, *Rebecca* and *Jamaica Inn* feature. A flock of crows perch menacingly on light fittings, a reminder of his 1963 thriller *The Birds*. The gents' toilet has stills of

room, the Grecian Saloon, was added in 1831. Magistrates refused it a licence, claiming it was '...resort of hundreds of profligate persons, where the utmost licentiousness prevailed.'

The Eagle remains a popular pub – happily free of licentiousness – and I enjoyed a pint of St Austell Proper Job alongside fellow customers, mainly office workers and students. Other real ales were Dark Star Partridge and Sharp's Doom Bar, plus Sandford's cider. With cast-iron pillars, a central mahogany bar, some ornate

*A silhouette of Alfred Hitchcock looks down from North by Northwest, though the film director would have known it as the North Pole. The pub is filled with posters and stills from his movies.*

Hitch's trademark cameo appearances in his films. I approached the pub after dark on a dank autumn night, when halos around street lights, ghostly clouds flitting across the sky and a reflective road surface combined to form a surreal, film-set appearance. The master of suspense would have approved.

Indoors, lighting is also moody. There are several separate areas, including a dining room and cosy corner with banquette seating and a wooden floor. Other ales on my visit included Timothy Taylor's Landlord and Fuller's London Pride. Outside terrace, meals, dog friendly.

**North by Northwest**, 188-190 New North Road, London, N1 7BJ. Tel. 0207 773 6660. www.northbynorthwestpub.com

## LONDON – LADBROKE GROVE
### A grave miscarriage of justice
### *Kensington Park Hotel ('KPH')*

Timothy Evans, a regular drinker here in the late 1940s, would still recognise this Victorian corner pub. He was found guilty and hanged in 1950 for the murder of his infant daughter Geraldine (and, by implication, that of his wife Beryl). Evans was posthumously pardoned in 1966. The murders were among several committed at 10 Rillington Place, probably all of them by infamous serial killer John Christie. Opposite is the library visited by Christie's wife on the day that Evans' wife Beryl was strangled. The 'KPH', as it is known, was among several Ladbroke Grove locations used for the 1971 film, *10 Rillington Place*, starring Sir Richard Attenborough as Christie and John Hurt as Evans. The KPH has other claims to fame. Singer Tom Jones made his London debut there in 1960; The Clash and Paul Weller have also performed; and, reputedly, the English fascist leader Oswald Mosley used it.

*The Kensington Park Hotel, or KPH, still contains its original island bar. It was used in the filming of 10 Rillington Place and Tom Jones made his London debut there.*

Sold in 2013, the KPH was under threat of permanent closure. Following a protest campaign, it was declared an 'asset of community value' and reopened in 2019, after a two-year refurbishment. Despite this makeover, heritage features such as a central island bar (circa 1890s); ornate, cast-iron columns and unusual window mouldings remain. The ales on offer are certainly superior to those of its earlier days as a Taylor Walker house: Thornbridge Lord Marples (ABV 4%), Timothy Taylor's Landlord (4.3%) and Harvey's Sussex Bitter (4%) when I called. A variety of photos illustrate past times when a venue for music and theatre but, unsurprisingly, I found no reminders of the Evans/Christie cases. Upstairs are spacious dining and function rooms and hotel accommodation.

Nearby: Don't miss the ornate, and Grade II listed, Elgin at 96 Ladbroke Grove.

*Kensington Park Hotel ('KPH')*, 139 Ladbroke Grove, Notting Hill, W10 6HJ. Tel. 0207 727 5876.
http://thekph.co.uk

## LONDON – LIMEHOUSE

### Described by Dickens and part-owned by McKellen

### *Grapes*

Colloquially known as 'Gandalf's pub' – it is part leased by actor Sir Ian McKellen, who made the part of Gandalf his own in the *Lord of the Rings* films – though it has a much longer history. McKellen, who lives nearby, used to be a customer, so when the landlady left, he decided to buy his local. He told the *London Evening Standard* of his strong link to the hospitality industry, born of an actor's long idle hours in hotels and other places of refreshment ('Sir Ian McKellen's grape expectations,' 12 January, 2012).

Charles Dickens frequented the Bunch of Grapes, as it was previously known, and he thinly disguised it as the Six Jolly Fellowship Porters* in *Our Mutual Friend*: 'A tavern of dropsical appearance…long settled down into a state of hale infirmity.' There has been a pub on the site since 1583. Oscar Wilde, in the *Picture of Dorian Gray* and Arthur Conan Doyle, in stories of *Sherlock Holmes*, also featured the area and would have known the pub – and the local opium dens of yore. The narrow building, dating from the 1720s, juts over the Thames. There are small wooden balconies on two levels, providing splendid views towards the towers of Canary Wharf. I also enjoyed watching the timeless progress of various river vessels.

Another customer of the Grapes was artist Antony Gormley. From the balcony, his sculpture of a lone man, perched atop a timber pile and installed in 2013, can be seen. Some perceive him as Old Father Thames but the artist calls his work *Another Time*; it is one of a hundred similar 'bodyforms' dispersed internationally. In Gormley's words: 'Each work is necessarily isolated and is an attempt to bear witness to what it is like to be alive and alone

*The Grapes in Limehouse was visited by Charles Dickens and featured it, as the Six Jolly Fellowship Porters, in one of his books.*

in space and time.' (www.antonygormley.com.) The work is contemporaneous with *Another Place*, his installation of men on the sands of the Mersey Estuary at Crosby Beach.

Inside, I found a proper local; a bare boards pub, busy with chatting customers and a fire blazing in the back room. The walls are hung with prints and local historical photos. As a winter-time dusk fell, I had a strong urge to 'hunker down' for a session. The selection of ales was a further inducement: Barth-Haas Hops Academy's Pale Ale (ABV 4.2%) was a surprising find and delicious; others included Black Sheep Bitter, St Austell Cornish Best and Timothy Taylor's Landlord. A fine beer, every one. Upstairs is a diminutive dining room. Dog friendly.

*Grapes*, 76 Narrow Street, London, E14 8BP.
Tel. 0207 987 4396. https://thegrapes.co.uk

* Some disagree: H.E. Popham, in *The Taverns of London* (1928) claims the location is the nearby Prospect of Whitby (below).

## LONDON – WAPPING (1)

### Visited by Pepys, Turner, royalty – and Hollywood stars

### *Prospect of Whitby*

At its peak as a dock thoroughfare, Wapping High Street had about 140 pubs, along with numerous houses of ill-repute, offering entertainment to the sailors. Of the few pubs that remain, we are lucky to have the Town of Ramsgate (q.v.) and this one, which claims to be the oldest surviving riverside hostelry. There has been one here since around 1520, making it 500 years old. It long had a reputation for villainy: so much so that an early name (after the Pelican) was the Devil's Tavern. Its customers were the river's riff-raff. (It burnt down in the eighteenth century and got its current name, and no doubt a better class of customer, on rebuilding.) Execution Dock was to the west, somewhere between the Town of Ramsgate pub and today's Wapping Overground station. Pirates,

*The Prospect of Whitby, seen from the river at low tide, claims to be the oldest surviving Thames-side pub. A replica gibbet and noose overlooks the shore, as a reminder of hangings of pirates and mutineers that took place nearby.*

smugglers and mutineers were hanged there, often watched by huge crowds, until as recently as 1830. A replica gibbet overhangs the river at the rear of the pub as a grim reminder of this – and that Judge Jeffries (the so-called 'hanging judge') was reputedly a customer. Diarist Samuel Pepys was another visitor, brought here by his job as Secretary to the Admiralty. Later, in 1839, artist J.M.W. Turner may have made sketches for *The Fighting Temeraire* from its riverside garden.

Bottle-glass bow windows grace the exterior while, inside, a flagstone floor, a pewter-topped bar supported on casks, wooden beams, ropes, lanterns and a spacious fireplace, contribute to a time-worn, maritime atmosphere. Climbing creaking steps to the upper floor is reminiscent of scaling the rigging of a man o'war; then you enter the Smugglers' Bar. This square, panelled room is where, if ghosts exist, they would surely reside. Across the hallway is the spacious Pepys Room for diners, with a riverside balcony. In its day, this was an upmarket restaurant frequented by the great and good. Princess Margaret, Prince Rainier and Hollywood stars dined here. Some are pictured in a portrait gallery: Richard Burton, Frank Sinatra and Judy Garland among them. The ale selection included examples from London breweries Twickenham and Sambrooks, along with Rock On from Hardys and Hansons and Abbott and IPA from Greene King. Courtyard garden, meals.

**Prospect of Whitby**, 57 Wapping Wall, Shadwell, London, E1W 3SH. Tel. 0207 481 1095.   www.greeneking-pubs.co.uk

## WAPPING (2)

### Where sailors and convicts were imprisoned
#### *Town of Ramsgate*

Wapping was home to the first London Docks, opened in 1805, but ships moored by Wapping Old Stairs (adjacent to this pub) hundreds of years before. So, the Ramsgate has a long history – it was established in 1545 – often being the 'last port of call' for sailors and shipborne passengers. The infamous Judge Jeffries (see Prospect of Whitby entry) supped there and was apprehended on its steps in the 1680s while trying to flee the country. Pirate Captain Kidd went to his death, as did many others, at nearby Execution Dock (no longer visible), in 1701. The pub's rear terraced garden looks across the river; I found it evocative to watch the waters lapping the shore, against steps used by generations of sailors. Its previous names include the Prince Of Denmark (1758), Ramsgate Old Town (1766) and it was unofficially known as the Red Cow, in honour of a popular barmaid's flaming red hair. Less romantic is

*The Town of Ramsgate has a long nautical history. Steps, reached via the adjacent passage, once led to a dock for sailing ships.*

the knowledge that the pub's cellars were used as cells, imprisoning men caught by the Royal Navy's press gangs so they didn't flee before being taken aboard ships. At other times, they held convicts awaiting transportation to America and, later, Australia.

The Town of Ramsgate, named after the Kentish fishermen who also used it, is long, narrow and cosy, with panelled walls and a lengthy bar counter. There are several information panels and old photos. I enjoyed a Harvey's Sussex Bitter, with other choices being Young's Bitter, Fuller's London Pride and Brains Festive Cheer. Many customers were availing themselves of a lunchtime meal but I was eager to continue by walking to the Prospect of Whitby. Ambient music.

**Town of Ramsgate**, 62, Wapping High Street, London E1W 2PN. Tel. 0207 481 8000. http://townoframsgate.pub

## LONDON – WEST END (1)

### Hub for bohemian Londoners until the 1950s

#### *Fitzroy Tavern*

*The ornate Fitzroy Tavern lent its name to a whole area – Fitzrovia – and has been superbly restored.*

The list of customers of this ornate establishment reads like a Who's Who: Dylan Thomas, George Orwell, Augustus John, Nina Hamnett (the flamboyant 'Queen of Bohemia'), Jacob Epstein, Richard Attenborough, Tommy Cooper and occultist Aleister Crowley among them. Its proximity to the BBC's Broadcasting House explains some but the 'Fitz', designed in 1897 by W.M. Brutton, pre-dates them all. It is the focal point of Fitzrovia, the area between Bloomsbury and Marylebone. From the 1920s to the '50s, it became the hub of London's bohemian set, growing in popularity and notoriety, thanks to its larger-than-life landlords. They welcomed writers, artists and others attracted by Fitzrovia's (then) low-rent accommodation. Photographer Robert Capa was a regular, who helped local children with toys and food parcels.

Its early beginnings were as a coffee house but it was converted to a pub in 1897 and gained its current moniker in 1919. For many years it was a tied Charrington's house. It was restored to its Victorian splendour by the current landlord, Yorkshire brewer Samuel Smith, winning a Pub Design award from CAMRA in 2018. Features include etched mirrors, engraved windows, polished panelling, real fires and a ceiling decorated with Lincrusta, an embossed linoleum invented in the 1870s. Ceramic tiling on walls and floors provides stately entrances, while the drinking areas are separated by glazed mahogany panels. A semi-island bar counter links six separate areas – you need to descend to basement level to cross between some. This subterranean passage contains a feast of information about the pub's colourful history. All drinks are from the Samuel Smith range (including Old Brewery Bitter) and there is a dining room upstairs.

*Fitzroy Tavern*, 16A Charlotte Street, London W1T 2LY. Tel. 0207 580 3714.

## WEST END (2)

### Hidden pub close to former 'Hellfire Club'

#### *Red Lion*

There are several Red Lions in this part of the capital – as the nation's most popular pub name that is hardly surprising – but this one is the trickiest to find. It is hidden in a narrow passageway (lit by antiquated gas lamps) that is variously home to a locksmith, the world's oldest hat shop (Lock & Co.) and diminutive cafés. The tavern emits a warm, inviting glow through its leaded windows. Its sign boasts 'Reputedly the second oldest licence in the West End, the village pub in the heart of St James's.' The L-shaped interior is small, decorated with framed prints and horse brasses – and contains an effigy of a red lion in a glazed cabinet. Bench seats are hard by panelled walls, while the counter is often crowded with customers drinking or ordering pints of Adnams Southwold, Courage Bitter or St Austell Tribute. Impossibly narrow staircases descend to the gents' toilet and climb to the Mirror Lounge, a tranquil sanctuary.

If the claim to be London's second oldest licensed premises is true, the Red Lion is at least 370 years old (the building itself is more recent). It may be even older – St James's was busy in Tudor times. There is a story that King Charles II's mistress, Nell Gwynne, used a secret tunnel from the cellar to nearby St James's Palace in order to cavort with her royal lover. This was debunked by Ted Bruning in *Historic Pubs of London*, saying the access point is more likely to be the entrance to a seventeenth-century cesspit. Its antiquity means it would have been known – and possibly visited – by members of the infamous Hellfire Club. This group of hedonists met on Sundays at different locations, with one popular venue being the Greyhound Tavern. The Greyhound is long gone but I discovered the Red Lion is just yards from its site. Founded in the early eighteenth century, the club had several rationales but (says Catharine Arnold in *City of Sin: London and its vices*) it was originally established to ridicule religion and conventional morality. Activities included dinners where members, dressed as characters from the Bible, turned up and ate 'Devil's loin' and 'Holy Ghost pie', washed down with lashings of Hell-fire punch. Those were the days.

It is likely that palace staff, even members of royalty, would have been among the Red Lion's customers. St James's Palace, just two minutes' walk, was where Charles II was born and where Charles I spent his last night, before his execution in 1649. Closed Sundays.

**Red Lion**, 23 Crown Passage (off Pall Mall), St James's, London SW1Y 6PP. Tel. 0207 930 4141.

## LYMINSTER, WEST SUSSEX
### A dragon-slayer's final drink
### *Six Bells*

This is home to a most bizarre folk tale. A nearby pool, Knucker Hole, said to be bottomless, was where a dragon, the Knucker, lived (p156, *A Companion to the Folklore, Myths & Customs of Britain*). The beast's nemesis turned out to be a farmer's boy, Jim Pulk. Instead of using a spear or crossbow as a weapon, he baked a huge pie laced with poison and carted it to the pool. The bait worked and master Pulk carried the dragon's severed head to the Six Bells for a celebratory pint. He drank up – and promptly died. According to the tale, some poison remained on his hand, contaminating his drink. The Slayer's Stone, or Slab, a Norman coffin lid in Lyminster church, is said to be from the boy's tomb; Knucker Hole can also be seen, now perfectly tranquil.

The 300-year-old, flint-built inn contains beams and an inglenook and is a short hop from the coast at Littlehampton. Real ales were from Fuller's and Sharp's and meals are served (separate dining area). Garden, dog friendly.

**Six Bells**, 168 Lyminster Road, BN17 7PS. Tel. 01903 713639. www.thesixbellslyminster.co.uk

*The Red Lion is one of the capital's most hidden pubs, situated in a gas-lit passage near St James's Palace.*

Hundreds of people, many in fancy dress, pit themselves against the thick mud and freezing waters of the Blackwater estuary once a year, while participating in the Maldon Mud Race. This gloop infused spectacle attracts thousands of spectators, along with photographers and television crews. Few know that the bizarre event began at a pub – the Queen's Head – which graces the waterside on the town's Hythe Quay, where Thames sailing barges are moored. It started in a small way in 1973, with a dare challenging the landlord to serve a meal on the saltings dressed in a dinner jacket. Following the success of this jape, the following year he opened a bar on the saltings. A score of people dashed across the river bed at low tide, downed a pint of beer and dashed back. The Maldon Mud Race was born.

*These competitors, who have reached the finish of the Maldon Mud Race after braving the gloop of the Blackwater estuary, are probably in need of a stiff drink.*

*The thousands who gather to watch or compete in the Maldon Mud Race each year are there because of the Queen's Head (centre, background) where it began as a dare for the landlord.*

It continued every year – often on Boxing Day or New Year's Day – until 1989, when it ceased due to a lack of facilities. But a new era would soon begin. A carnival association was formed and the event restarted in 1994, based in Promenade Park, a short stroll from the pub. It is now held in spring, when better weather attracts greater participation and sponsorship. In 2017, more than £35,000 was distributed to various good causes.

The pub was serving six ales, including Dark Star Hophead, Adnams Ghost Ship and, maintaining its tradition of stocking

Essex microbrews, there was Bishop Nick's Ridley's Rite (3.6% ABV) and the moreish Puck's Folly (4.2%) from Maldon Brewing Company. The beer menu was detailed on a blackboard. The interior resembles 'below deck' on a sailing ship, with a shiplap-fringed central servery, wood floors, bench seating and brass fittings. There are two compact bars, a separate dining room (the Port Hole) and outdoor seating on the quayside. A framed poster of the race held in 1982 has pride of place and is captioned 'Birthplace of the Maldon Mud Race'. Elsewhere are historical photos with a local and nautical flavour. Though I was there early on the morning of the Mud Race, there were already plenty of customers and an atmosphere of eager anticipation. The tide slowly receded, revealing the slimy and glutinous conditions so vital to the day's success. Meals, ambient music, dog friendly, newspapers.

Nearby: Maldon is also home to the Mighty Oak Brewery – check out their brewery tap, the Tap Room, in High Street and Farmer's Yard micro-pub.

**Queen's Head**, The Hythe, CM9 5HN. Tel. 01621 854112. thequeensheadmaldon.co.uk

## MANCHESTER, GREATER MANCHESTER (1)
### The pubs that moved – twice!
### *Old Wellington and Sinclair's Oyster Bar*

These two timber-framed pubs, adjacent (but independent) businesses near the Cathedral, have been moved twice in living memory. Known collectively as The Shambles, they comprise the Old Wellington (among the city's oldest buildings, dating from the mid sixteenth century, though only a pub since 1830) and Sinclair's, originally a gentlemen's club (*circa* 1730). They were initially situated between St Mary's Gate and Cateaton Street. They had to be raised by almost 5 feet in the 1970s, to accommodate access to the Arndale Centre. Then, in 1996, the city centre was shattered

*In an incredible feat of engineering, Manchester's Old Wellington and Sinclair's Oyster Bar were moved a hundred metres to their current site near the city's cathedral.*

*This Edwardian postcard shows the Wellington in its original location and looking quite run-down.*

by an IRA bomb; the whole area was subsequently redeveloped. It was decided, somewhat controversially, to move the pair – lock, stock and barrel – a hundred metres to this new site, where they reopened less than three years later. It was a herculean task – like a giant, three-dimensional jigsaw puzzle – but the builders did a perfect job.

The Old Wellington, part of the Nicholson's chain, offers a wide choice of ales (seven on my visit, including bitters from Green Jack and Skinner's). The upper dining area is a veritable forest of beams while, downstairs, is a plaque to poet John Byrom. Born in the building in 1692, he pioneered an early form of shorthand. The labyrinthine Sinclair's is a Samuel Smith house, serving only the Yorkshire brewery's branded drinks and no real ale. Both pubs serve meals and share outside seating.

**Old Wellington**, 4 Cathedral Gates, M3 1SW.
Tel. 0161 839 5179. www.nicholsonspubs.co.uk
**Sinclair's Oyster Bar**, 2 Cathedral Gates, M3 1SW.
Tel. 0161 834 0430.

## MANCHESTER (MIDDLETON), GREATER MANCHESTER (2)

### Meetings of radicals before the Peterloo Massacre

### *Olde Boar's Head*

Entering this aged, timber-framed inn is like boarding a Tudor galleon. There are no straight lines, just time-worn beams, creaking floors and – upstairs – names of otherwise forgotten individuals, scratched into ageing plaster. A rare Grade II* listed pub, it is one of the oldest intact public houses in England, though it probably began as a pair of clothiers' houses, merged for the purpose of hospitality. Part of its timber framing has been tree-ring dated, which confirms a date of 1622. The first tenant was Isaac Walkden, whose tenure was brief: he died during a typhus

*The Olde Boar's Head, Middleton, is an incredible survivor whose first tenant died of typhus in 1623.*

epidemic in summer, 1623 (his will is preserved at Lancashire Archives). The building consists of five oak bays, all locked together with oak pegs like a medieval assembly kit. The wall-frames were filled with wattle and daub, an example of which survives in the bar area.

During the eighteenth and nineteenth centuries, the tavern was the hub of its community, a venue for political and public meetings. Travelling Justices of the Peace presided over court sessions in the Sessions Room; while less respectable prize fighting tournaments were staged in the barn. This remarkable place was taken over by Manchester brewery J. W. Lees, who carried out a meticulous restoration in 1988. During the works, a child's shoe was discovered behind the stairs and examined before being carefully replaced. (Shoes were often placed in medieval houses as good luck tokens.) I enjoyed a pint of Lees Bitter (ABV 4%) as local historian Geoff Wellens took me on an impromptu tour. Upstairs, he showed me the Meeting Room with its heavy door, and marks made by superstitious carpenters – either to ward off evil spirits or protect against fire; possibly both. They have been carefully burned on to the wooden mullions with a lit taper.

A cosy snug bears the title 'Sam Bamford's Room': it was here that the political radical and poet held court, later leading a band of his neighbours to an infamous Manchester demonstration of 1819. Its violent break-up by soldiers led to it being named the Peterloo Massacre. It seems the Boar's Head was the 'local' for generations of Bamfords, as Sam writes of his father flooring an opponent in a prize-fight and his grandfather joining the Pretender's (Bonnie Prince Charlie's) Party in the pub – for which he was arrested for treason. Meals, garden.

**Olde Boar's Head,** 111 Long Street, Middleton, M24 6UE. Tel. 0161 643 0076.
www.jwlees.co.uk/locations/the-olde-boars-head

## MARFORD, WREXHAM
### The 'haunted village' and a window-tapper
### *Trevor Arms*

*Focal point of the 'haunted village' of Marford, the Trevor Arms features Gothic windows and crucifixes set into walls.*

The houses of Marford look as though they were designed by a *Hammer Horror* set designer; or at least a flamboyant architect with a fixation on the Gothic. Windows are strangely shaped, roofs sinuous and there are even crucifixes hollowed into walls. Several crucifixes decorate the rear of this nineteenth-century coaching inn. The old stable block (now guest accommodation) has windows in the shape of eyes – a feature seen elsewhere in the village. They seemed to follow us across the car park, into the pub with its black-lined, ogee-shaped windows and stately sign bearing the Trevalyn crest. An employee, Megan Davies, explained that Marford is known as a haunted village and the crosses are to protect people from the wandering spirit of 'Lady Blackbird', aka Margaret Blackbourne. She was murdered by her husband George, steward of the Trevalyn estate, in 1713. According to legend, a verdict of misadventure was decided by the magistrate. George soon took another wife. Margaret is said to tap at windows in search of her husband and his new bride. The pub is also reputedly haunted, though not necessarily by Margaret. Megan told me she has glimpsed the ghost of a male figure – and paranormal groups have been to investigate the building.

Perhaps of more interest, to sceptical readers at least, is the fact that this was the favourite pub of an RAF pilot whose exploits were dramatized in the film *The Great Escape*. According to Welsh history website *Historypoints.org*, Ken Rees had his bachelor party here, in 1942. Soon afterwards, his bomber was shot down over Norway and he was imprisoned in Stalag Luft III, where he helped build its famous escape tunnel. Though he failed to flee the POW camp, he survived the war and went on to run a night-club on Anglesey.

I enjoyed a pint of Bath Ales' Summer Hare (ABV 3.9%), with St Austell Tribute and Caledonian Golden XPA also on hand-pull. The interior is labyrinthine, comfortable and mainly set for diners. It continues the exterior's black-and-white décor, with some gnarled beams. Other historical features are lacking, though the log fire is a good place to gather around for ghost stories, no doubt. Meals, accommodation, outdoor seating. Served by buses from Wrexham.

**Trevor Arms**, Marford Hill, LL12 8TA. Tel. 01244 579418.
trevorarms-marford.com

## MUSSELBURGH, LOTHIAN

### A customer in flames
### *Volunteer Arms (Staggs)*

This popular bar has been in the same family for 160 years – its first licensee, Edinburgh brewer James MacKell Montgomery, was born in 1831; the building dates from 1858. It is a consistent CAMRA award winner, being named National Pub of the Year in 1998 and, more recently, in 2018. It received a 'Best in the Lothians' award 25 times, and the Edinburgh and South East Scotland title eight times. At least 28 of these award certificates are displayed in a corner of the panelled bar and snug, which also boasts some vintage

*Customers in the wood-panelled Volunteer Arms, Musselburgh look more at ease today than the one who set himself alight in the 1950s.*

brewery mirrors. The bar was packed, with mixed groups, couples and individuals, at 6pm on a Friday evening.

My request to busy landlord Nigel Finlay for some historical information resulted in a well-thumbed copy of Jim Lawrie's *Staggs – A History of Fisherrow's Volunteer Arms* (Spiderwize.com, 2013). Perhaps the most startling of the anecdotes within its pages is that of a local motor mechanic who called in for a beer one lunchtime in the 1950s. He wore overalls saturated with oil and grease. Sipping his pint, he then proceeded to light a pipe (smoking in bars then being a popular activity) but was promptly engulfed in flames. Two customers came to his aid, using jugs of cask-conditioned Campbell's ale. The unnamed man was saved from injury but 'a little put out', to quote the author.

A regularly changing menu of real ales is chalked on a blackboard. These included three from Oakham: JHB, Bishop's Farewell and Citra; Fine Ales' Jarl; Swannay Pale, Cromarty Red Rocker and Loch Lomond Silkie Stout. On CAMRA's Regional Inventory (look out for the four vintage spirit casks sitting atop the old bar gantry). Dog friendly, outdoor area, traditional games. Popular with racegoers at Musselburgh.

*Staggs*, 81 North High Street, EH21 6JE. Tel. 0131 665 9654. www.staggsbar.com

## MYTHOLMROYD, WEST YORKSHIRE

### The Cragg Vale Coiners
### *Hinchliffe Arms*

This stone-built gem is hidden off the main road, between folds of hills. To reach it, you drive or take the bus up England's longest continuous gradient (an official roadside sign tells you so); the route of the Tour de France when it visited Yorkshire. Few outside the area have heard of the gang known as the Cragg Vale Coiners. Theirs is a story of forgery, intimidation and murder that could serve as the script of a Hollywood blockbuster. This pub, built

*Hidden amid the rugged scenery of Cragg Vale, the Hinchliffe Arms is a welcome oasis, known for its good ale and food.*

*circa* 1905, has a contemporary interior. It wasn't extant in the Coiners' day, but is on the site of the Cragg Vale Inn, dating from the early 1700s, which they would have known. The original cellar is still in use and the barman told me it has a stream running through it. There are three real ales, all from the J.W. Lees stable, including house beer The Hinch (ABV 3.7%) and a menu which attracts diners from a wide area. In the inn's day, it lay in the shadow of a towering mill belonging to cotton spinners' Hinchliffe & Sons; today its only lofty neighbour is a church, St John the Baptist in the Wilderness.

In the eighteenth century, 'coining' – devaluing the currency by clipping coins, melting the offcuts and counterfeiting new ones – was an established racket in the area. Cragg Vale became its epicentre in the 1760s, thanks to its remoteness and the ruthlessness of master forger 'King' David Hartley. Many local people were involved and Hartley boasted about his exploits in the taverns. His family's isolated farmhouse, Bell House, can still be seen. The local excise man, William Deighton, persuaded a gang member to inform on his leader, enabling him to serve a warrant on Hartley in the Old Cock Inn, Halifax. (Pubs feature strongly in this story.) Deighton was then murdered by two 'hit men' hired by Hartley's brother; they were acquitted through lack of evidence. 'King' David did not escape the hangman, however. He was found guilty of coining and executed in York in 1770.

Outside seating, usually accompanied by the cluck of foraging chickens, and the sound of the fast-flowing Elphin Brook. Dog friendly, real fire.

Nearby: Hartley's grave can be seen in the hill-top village of Heptonstall. You can also walk the scenic Cragg Vale Heritage Trail, with its information panels, one of which is outside the Hinchliffe. A shorter riverside walk takes you from the pub to the Robin Hood in Cragg Road, a popular community local that has won plaudits from CAMRA.

**Hinchliffe Arms**, Church Bank Lane, Cragg Vale (near Hebden Bridge), HX7 5TA. Tel. 01422 883256. https://thehinchliffe.co.uk

## NEAR SAWREY, CUMBRIA
### Beatrix Potter's local
### *Tower Bank Arms*

This diminutive inn, dating from the seventeenth century, is immortalized in the pages of *Jemima Puddle-Duck*. One of Beatrix Potter's (1866-1943) illustrated children's books, it has never been out of print. Surrounded by stunning Lake District scenery and adjacent to her beloved farm and house, Hill Top, the location is sublime. Stepping inside on a bright autumn day, my happiness multiplied. There is a traditional oaken bar, the counter lined with a pleasing array of Cumbrian ales; and a blazing log fire and range, surrounded by wooden chairs and settles. A slate floor, heavy oak beams, a dartboard and grandfather clock complete the bucolic scene. Like Hill Top itself and much of the surrounding

*Decorative hand-pulls on the oaken bar of the Tower Bank Arms promise some superb ales, as a fire blazes in the background.*

land, the Tower Bank Arms is owned by the National Trust. Potter bequeathed everything to the charity: she is credited for preserving much of what is now the Lake District National Park. She didn't own this property, however and there's doubt as to whether she even crossed the threshold. 'We get asked that a lot,' said the barman. 'We don't know for sure. She disapproved of alcohol and may have been teetotal.'

According to publican's daughter Willow Taylor, born in 1913 and one of the last people to remember her locally, she wasn't a fan of youngsters either. Willow's parents ran the pub and she would see Beatrix from time to time as she was growing up. 'Crabby old thing, we used to think. She didn't stop or chat to us, she wasn't all that fond of children…they were a bit of a nuisance.' (p.64, Robinson-Tate and Rigby, *Lake District Icons*, History Press, 2014.) As I sat by the fire with my pint of Hawkshead Bitter, I wondered what Potter would have made of the pile of her books alongside a stash of well-thumbed pub and beer guides.

Aside from two Hawkshead ales, there was Loweswater Gold and Langdale from Cumbrian Legendary Ales, Tag Lag from Barngates at the Drunken Duck (q.v.) and a variety of scrumpy ciders: no wonder the pub has won awards from CAMRA. Food is important (there is a Victorian dining room) but drinkers aren't neglected. I met a hiker from Kendal who has been calling in for a pint regularly over the past twenty-five years. He told me about the time he saw two tourists from the US come in, late one evening, eulogizing about the lovely countryside. Assuming they'd been touring the Lakes, the landlord asked where they'd been. 'We've been to Colchester, it was fantastic,' they replied. Open-mouthed, the publican checked they meant the Essex town, a round-trip of 630 miles. 'Yes, we've been to see friends. It was quite a long way and boy we were glad to get back to this hotel tonight.' Meals (book for dinner), garden (with views), accommodation, dog friendly.

Nearby: Beatrix Potter's Hill Top (National Trust). Good walks and cycle rides.

**Tower Bank Arms**, LA22 0LF. Tel. 015394 36334.
www.towerbankarms.co.uk

## NORWICH, NORFOLK (1)

### A soldier's deathbed and a smuggling landlady
### *Adam and Eve*

A beer house stood on the same spot as long ago as 1249, built by monks around a well in the cellar. The latter has been converted into a cave-like basement bar. The monks were brewers and paid workers building the city's cathedral in bread and ale. The brick and flint building, with its flagstone floors and twin bars was scene of an army officer's death during a medieval battle for the city. The unfortunate officer was Lord Sheffield of the King's Army, who was mortally wounded during a peasants' uprising, Kett's Rebellion (1549). He was carried by his comrades to the pub, where he died (and is one of the hostelry's several reputed ghosts).

*The Adam and Eve in Norwich started as a beer house run by monks. It was a refuge during a local uprising.*

Three hundred years later, in the 1850s, the Adam and Eve was run by a landlady with a smuggling sideline. Elizabeth Howes (née Thurling) also owned a wherry that carried cargoes of sand from the coast. This was sold to pubs for use on floors and in spittoons. These shipments were used to conceal smuggled liquor. She would have found no shortage of customers for these cut-price spirits, apparently doing a roaring trade. It was then a rather rough pub, frequented by bargemen.

Today's customers are a mixture of locals and tourists. The place is small and cosy, usually busy and always atmospheric. Seating is on antique settles and Windsor chairs. There are crooked beams and historical photos. Four ales on my visit: the quaffable Wolf Golden Jackal (ABV 3.9%), Adnams Southwold Bitter, Greene King St. Edmunds and the full-bodied Theakston's Old Peculier (5.6%). Meals, ambient music, outside seating. On CAMRA's Regional Inventory.

**Adam and Eve**, 17 Bishopgate, NR3 1RZ.
Tel. 01603 667423.

## NORWICH, NORFOLK (2)
### Site of medieval executions
### *Lollards Pit (formerly Bridge House)*

This largely seventeenth-century pub, with earlier features, stands on the site of the eponymous pit, where heretics were executed during past centuries. A plaque by the door proclaims the morbid fact and, for a long time, the area was shunned by people because of this macabre past. Eventually, a building was erected, possibly as part of a tannery, then becoming the city's first pub east of the River Wensum. It was always known colloquially as Lollards Pit, so when new owners took over the Bridge House and began to restore it, they adopted the name. Though rooms have been opened out, rough-hewn beams are much in evidence, as well as old fireplaces (with wood-burning stoves). A patio garden features an ancient well.

I was able to choose from five Norfolk ales, including examples from Moongazer, Panther, Wild Craft and Woodforde's breweries. An informative exhibit explains that the pit was owned by the Bishop of Norwich and excavated to provide cathedral foundation material. During religious persecutions, it was seen as an appropriate site for burnings – more than 40 during the reign of Queen 'Bloody' Mary (1553-58) alone. Many were 'Lollards', that is reformers who believed the Church was corrupt. The barman explained that customers have come from as far as New Zealand, as they have discovered an ancestor who came to an awful end here. Snacks, pub games, dog friendly, ambient music.

**Lollards Pit**, 69-71 Riverside Road, NR1 1SR.
Tel. 01603 624675. https://lollards-pit-pub.ueniweb.com

*Lollard's Pit, Norwich, stands on the site of an execution place for heretics. It attracts customers from around the world, following in the footsteps of ancestors who died there.*

## OXFORD, OXFORDSHIRE

### A house of mechanical wonders – and a giant

### *Chequers*

*Chequers in Oxford is reached via a narrow alleyway and courtyard garden. It once housed an animal menagerie.*

Arguably the university city's most hidden pub – it is reached via a cobbled alleyway, off High Street. A jumble of buildings along this snickelway were once tenements, and the home of a money lender (the Roman sign for which was a chequerboard) but the area is now occupied by this deceptively large, twin-level pub. The Chequers was first mentioned in 1605, when a draper, John Greene, was given a licence to keep an inn. Carved stonework around one of the fireplaces looks original, though most of the beams are much more recent. The lofty, quarry-tiled downstairs bar is characterful and there is a barn-like, stone dining room, upstairs. The inn was entrepreneurial from its early days, doubling as an exhibition hall. For about a century from 1680, it housed a collection of mechanical equipment, before diversifying into zoological curiosities. The inventions on show included a spit that could roast six dishes at once and a loom titled 'Nevill's New Woollen Machine'. The menagerie, in place by 1762, comprised 14 large animals including a camel, sealion, racoon, an unidentified marsupial and 'a large fish'.

After three years, the novelty of wild creatures had presumably worn off. The display was changed to a fire engine and 'new type of candlestick'. By 1776, a giant from Hertfordshire had become the main attraction: so popular was he that he was invited to dine at various colleges. Sadly, there is no evidence of the inn's myriad of past exhibits, though I was puzzled by a curious mechanical object in a tall, varnished box fixed to the wall. This, it transpires, is an ordinary wood-case clock minus its clock-face. "It fell off one day, almost hitting a customer, so it's awaiting repair," said an apologetic staff member. Being part of the Nicholson's chain, I found an excellent range of nine real ales on ten handpumps – including the house beer, Nicholson's Pale Ale (ABV 4%), brewed by St Austell, plus examples from Thornbridge, Five Points, London Brewing, Jaw Brew, Sharp's and Brakspear. On my visit there were plenty of customers, particularly in the cobbled courtyard. The absence of 'curiosities' seems not to have harmed business. Meals, ambient music, board games, dog friendly.

***Chequers***, 130a High Street, OX1 4DH. Tel. 01865 727463. www.nicholsonspubs.co.uk

## OXFORD (HEADINGTON), OXFORDSHIRE

### Joan of Headington – a game girl
### *White Hart*

I called at this seventeenth-century pub while on a bicycle ride around Oxford. My exertions climbing Headington Hill were well rewarded with a pint of dry-hopped Everard's Tiger and a hearty Sunday roast (pies were another menu speciality). In its early days, academics scaled the same hill and strolled to the alehouse for more than beer and food. It is believed to be the inn then known as Joan's of Headington, a brothel beyond the jurisdiction of the university, run by the eponymous madame. It features in a play by William King, a Doctor of Civil Law at Christ Church, called *The Tragi-Comedy of Joan of Hedington* (sic), published in *Useful Miscellanies* in 1712. Photographs of the original publication are framed beside the bar, indicating the White Hart is not ashamed of its salacious past. The rumbustious story ends with Joan being hanged by an angry client of Mother Harris, a prostitute she has insulted. The 'Topping Dame of Hedington' is rescued in the nick of time – by her husband.

*Set in stone-built terrace, Headington's White Hart was once run by an infamous landlady.*

The Grade II listed, stone-built alehouse had become more respectable by 1750, when it was given its current name, and was acquired by Hall's Brewery in 1829. It is now part of Leicestershire brewer Everard's estate. It was also the annual meeting place for the South Oxfordshire Hounds, having stabling for six horses at the rear (the stables can be seen at the end of the garden).

The multi-roomed hostelry has two bars, part flag-stoned and part wood-floored, punctuated by steps up and down to the seating areas. Panelled walls, beams, stoves and local prints complement the historical atmosphere. A collection of board games included the intriguing *Worst Case Scenario Survival Game*, which I'm sure Joan would have been up for playing. Ales from Everard's (Tiger and Sunchaser), Castle Rock, Brunswick Brewing and Lacons, plus two real ciders. CAMRA Oxford city pub of the year, 2013 and 2017. Ambient music, occasional live music.

Nearby: Look out for the Headington Shark, a quirky sculpture that protrudes from the roof of a house.

*White Hart*, 12 St Andrew's Road, Headington, OX3 9DL. Tel. 01865 761737. https://thewhitehartheadington.com

## PAINSWICK, GLOUCESTERSHIRE

### 99 yews and puppy-dog pie
### *Falcon Hotel*

Across the road from this former coaching inn is a sight that attracts camera-toting tourists from around the world. St Mary's churchyard has row upon row of neatly-clipped yew trees. Legend says there are 99 and no more can ever grow, but others can't agree on numbers. On the Sunday nearest 19 September, local children perform a dance and procession around the yews known as 'Clypping the Church' (an old English word for embracing). Even more unusual is the tradition of dining on 'puppy-dog pie'. An old tale is of visitors to the Falcon being served a dish of cooked puppy, as the landlord had no food (the guests were from Stroud

The Falcon is spacious, its rooms laid mainly for dining but there is a pleasingly simple bar, complete with wood floor, stove and high-back settles, among an assortment of wooden furniture. I enjoyed a pint of GWB Maiden Voyage Bitter (ABV 4%), though it was a tough choice between that and Hook Norton Hooky or Wye Valley HPA. There's also local cider and a gin menu.

Dating from 1554 but rebuilt 1711, the Falcon is a focal point of the town: a one-time squire's court and home to cock-fighting that continued even after the activity was outlawed in 1830. Courtyard garden, accommodation.

*Falcon Hotel*, New Street, GL6 6UN. Tel. 01452 814222. www.falconinn-cotswolds.co.uk

## PANGBOURNE, BERKSHIRE
### A pub in two counties
### *Swan*

We are fortunate to have liberal licensing hours in this country, but it wasn't always the case. Older readers may remember when they were restricted and sometimes varied between counties or districts. Such was the case in Berkshire and Oxfordshire; a confusing situation as this Thames-side hostelry straddled the county boundary. The then landlord used this bureaucratic quirk to everyone's advantage. When he called 'time, gentlemen', regulars used it as a cue to move to an adjacent part of the rambling inn. There they continued drinking, perfectly legally, for another half-hour. The Swan is one of several riverside establishments mentioned in Jerome K. Jerome's humorous travelogue *Three Men in a Boat*, published in 1889. Humour turned to melancholy soon after the three boaters departed, as they witnessed a female suicide victim in the water. The pub would also have been known to Kenneth Grahame, author of *Wind in the Willows*, who retired to the village after a career at the Bank of England.

*The Falcon Hotel once reputedly sold puppy-dog pie. The Painswick locals were known as 'bow-wows.'*

and there's historic rivalry between the two towns). Whether the story is true or not, those Painswick born-and-bred are known as 'bow-wows'. These days, the pie – if you are able to track one down – is a beef and vegetable version, with a dog-shaped china vent in the middle. When I asked the landlord if he had it on the menu he replied, nonchalantly, 'Not anymore,' as if he is asked the question several times every day. 'The last owner took the recipe with him. You need to go to the Royal Oak.' Down at the Oak the barmaid looked perplexed. 'I remember a sign outside advertising such a pie but they've not sold it since I've been here. It doesn't sound very appetizing.'

*Customers at the Swan in Pangbourne enjoy the riverside ambience, oblivious to the fact there was once a nightly farce when last orders were called.*

## PENALLT, MONMOUTHSHIRE

### Dead men do talk

### *Boat Inn*

An inn was established here circa 1642, during the Civil War, to refresh artillery units guarding the river crossing. Though the Grade II listed, flint and brick building is much altered, there are many clues to its history. These include nooks and crannies at different levels, oak beams, floors of flagstone, brick and wood and a very old fireplace. A long, central room – which houses the bar counter – resembles a medieval hall, opening onto a riverside terrace with mooring for customers. A sunken room has been converted from a coal-bunker. Though catering well for diners, there are several cosy areas for drinkers. I had a choice between five real ales: two from Mad Squirrel – Hopfest Pale (ABV 3.8%) and Resolution (4.2%) – Hogs Back TEA (4.2%), Greene King IPA (3.6%) and Abbott (5%). Dog friendly, ambient music, occasional live music, board games, limited parking. Nearby: This is a good refreshment stop on the Thames Path.

**Swan**, Shooters Hill, RG8 7DU. Tel. 0118 984 4494.
www.swanpangbourne.co.uk

To reach this stone-built, time-worn Welsh hostelry, it's best to park in England (Redbrook, Gloucestershire) and cross the River Wye into the principality. One can do this using an old iron bridge that carried the Wye Valley Railway until its closure in 1964. Its setting is a wooded cliff, of which the inn seems a natural appendage. A terraced garden climbs the hillside by means of leafy terraces, with a waterfall cascading down. Sitting here, watching the canoeists below, is only matched by 'front-row' seats, on benches along the riverbank itself. Penallt is accessed via steep lanes and there is a story that pall-bearers would rest at a special 'coffin seat' when carrying deceased locals to church. On one memorable occasion, a funeral party, fortified by ale, rested at the appointed seat with the corpse of a wealthy but miserly farmer. They were refreshing themselves with more drink when the dead man suddenly sat bolt upright and calmly asked for a drink of water. When he finally did pass away, according to the tale, his widow instructed the pall-bearers they were not to stop but instead go straight to the churchyard. Spring water tumbling through the Boat's garden was once piped across the river to be used by the long closed Redbrook Brewery.

The slate-floored bar, with whitewashed stone walls, has a rustic counter in half-timbered style. Beer casks and cider boxes are stacked behind, along with jars of pickled eggs (there are no handpumps and, apparently, no cellar). I enjoyed a Wickwar Mole's Gold (ABV 3.8%) with Wye Valley Butty Bach (4.5%) the tempting alternative. This is also a cider pub: I counted 12 listed on a blackboard headed 'cheaper than therapy'. There are solid fuel stoves and a selection of traditional games for times when the weather is inclement. A notice informed customers that the pub was for sale. On enquiring whether this would mean closure, the bar lady reassured me that 'this pub would never shut down

– there would be an outcry.' I would certainly be among the first to cry out. Of interest to railway enthusiasts: there was once a halt near the pub and the distance between it and the next, at Redbrook, is believed to have been the shortest between two stops on the national network. Meals, real fire, dog friendly.

Nearby: The Wye Valley Walk passes the pub.

**Boat Inn**, Lone Lane, near Monmouth, NP25 4AJ (car park satnav NP25 4LZ). Tel. 01600 712615. www.theboatpenallt.co.uk

*Beer is served from the cask at the Boat Inn, which once piped its spring water across the river to the local brewery.*

## PERTH, PERTH & KINROSS
### Murder of a Scottish king
### *King James (formerly Christies Bar)*

The Fair City could have become the capital of Scotland but its image was blackened in 1437, when King James I of Scotland was assassinated in a failed coup. His wife, Queen Joan, was wounded but escaped. Blackfriars monastery, where the deed occurred – it was used a royal residence – has gone but this pub is believed to occupy part of the site. I was able to gaze through an observation window at thirteenth-century foundations in the cellar. The viewpoint is set into the floor beside an island bar. There are information panels giving details of an archaeological dig of 2017, when the discovery was made. The pub was being refurbished at the time and its decoration is contemporary. There was no real ale but keg beers include Belhaven Best and Greene King East Coast IPA. Lunchtime meals, ambient music, pool table.

*King James*, 73 Kinnoull Street, PH1 5EZ.
Tel. 01738 637656.

## PETERBOROUGH, CAMBRIDGESHIRE
### War memorial in the public bar
### *Hand and Heart*

Wreath-laying and prayers at war memorials are common on Armistice Day but only rarely do ceremonies take place inside a pub. Just such a Remembrance Service was held on 12 November, 2017, in the public bar of this back-street gem, built in 1938. The city's mayor, mayoress and other local dignitaries accompanied staff and regulars beside the hostelry's war memorial. Situated on a wall of the main bar, the shiny brass plaque pays tribute to those killed and missing in World War Two. I found it garlanded with Lady Haig poppies. It was erected by subscription and has seen regular commemorations, though none since the above event, according to the barman.

A free house since 2016, it is the only pub in the county listed on CAMRA's National Inventory. This is thanks to its original 'Moderne' style bar counter, bar-back and fixed bench seating, all in perfect condition. At the rear is a smoke room, complete with its hatch for service. I found a selection of six real ales, which change regularly. I supped a pleasing D.J. Robot IPA from Rockingham (3.9% ABV), with other options being Revolutions Meat is Murder, Tydd Steam Broken Brexit, Brewsters Decadence and two stouts: Renown Loveleigh Cockle Stout and Czars P2 Imperial (8% ABV). Busy with regulars on a cold Saturday afternoon, there was a friendly welcome and I enjoyed watching a darts game. Crib and dominoes are also played. Regular live music, dog friendly, real fire, garden.

*Hand and Heart*, 12 Highbury Street, PE1 3BE.
Tel. 01733 564653.

*The war memorial in the front bar of the Hand and Heart, Peterborough. It is also known for its wide-ranging selection of real ale.*

## PICKERING, NORTH YORKSHIRE

### A railway's birthplace – serving 'train beers'
### *Black Swan*

Many visitors to this market town arrive in style, by steam train, on the North Yorkshire Moors Railway. This former coaching inn, dating from 1740 and once owned by Braims Brewery of Tadcaster, is not only pivotal in the NYMR's history, but home to a train-themed microbrewery. A plaque explains that when the Whitby & Pickering Railway, as it was called, opened in May 1836, a 300-strong celebratory procession walked to the Black Swan 'for a collation'. There was cheering from thousands of onlookers; cannons were fired and brass bands played. The plaque dates from the line's reopening (as a heritage railway) 137 years later. It was unveiled by HRH The Duchess of Kent.

The brewery, Great British Breworks, whose beers 'take their character from aspects of great railways of the world' opened, in a stone-built wash-house, in 2016. I was able to choose between Orient Express Istanbul Pale (ABV 4.3%), Great Scot 70/- Heavy (3.8%), Lydney Coal Porter (4.9%), and two other Yorkshire brewers' beers, including Timothy Taylor's Landlord. Despite the above history, do not expect an 'olde worlde' inn, as – apart from an impressive stone wall and some ageing timbers – the establishment has been modernized. The two main rooms combine to form a cavernous space, ideal for regular live music and other events. There is a chrome-topped, sinuous bar counter and vintage radios are dotted around for decoration. Diners are well catered for, though this is also a drinkers' pub. There is outdoor seating in the former stable yard where, in 1910, a horse-drawn hearse was available for hire. Accommodation, cocktail bar, dog friendly, real fire, ambient music.

Nearby: This is a town of inns. The Sun Inn, Westgate, has been declared the local CAMRA Pub of the Year on many occasions, holds regular acoustic music nights and matches on its two Petanque courts. The Bay Horse Inn, Market Place, is a former

*Plaque outside Pickering's Black Swan, focal point of celebrations on the opening of the North Yorkshire Moors Railway.*

coaching inn where Roundhead soldiers were billeted during the Civil War. There is a fireside hidey-hole, reputedly used by Cromwell, in the front bar.

*Black Swan*, 18 Birdgate, YO18 7AL. Tel. 01751 798209. www.blackswan-pickering.co.uk

## PRESTON, HERTFORDSHIRE

### The first pub co-operative
### *Red Lion*

When locals heard their beloved pub, dating from the 1840s and beside the village green, was going to be revamped and turned into a steakhouse by Whitbread, they didn't just moan. Ninety-two of them got together and bought the place, lock stock and barrel, reopening it as their 'perfect local'. That was in 1983, more than thirty-six years ago. It was the first pub co-operative in Britain; a prime example of 'people power', setting a blueprint for many

During my visit, locals were toasting it being voted local CAMRA Pub of the Year, meaning Harry can rest easy. (It was later included in a shortlist of four in the running to be National Pub of the Year.) A letter from Queen Elizabeth the Queen Mother says how impressed she was with 'the citizens of Preston creating a happy meeting place.' Home cooked food is part of the offer, as are board games, a dartboard, a library of books and magazines, the absence of ambient music and a spacious garden, full of lupins and marguerites. A Union Flag fluttered outside the Georgian building, with its twin red front doors. Dog friendly, occasional live music.

Nearby: This is a good area for walking and cycling.

***Red Lion***, The Green, near Hitchin, SG4 7UD. Tel. 01462 459585. www.theredlionpreston.co.uk

*The Red Lion in Preston, Hertfordshire was the first pub to be bought by its customers. It made the shortlist for CAMRA's National Pub of the Year.*

## PRIOR'S DEAN, HAMPSHIRE
### The Pub With No Name
### *White Horse*

hostelry-rescues that followed. In an age when dozens are closing, the Red Lion continues to thrive. It's the sort of place where you instantly feel at home. Today, local shareholders, led by their Board of Directors, still have a say in how it is run. Some helped with the original redecoration – the polished wooden bar was made 'from a kit and an old church pew', while others helped 'hang enough wallpaper to cover the village green.'

A splendid selection of five ales (along with real cider) included Tring Brewery's Side Pocket for a Toad (ABV 3.6%), Kent Brewery's New Black APA (4.8%) and Milton Apollo (6%). In the main bar, decorated with dried hops and warmed by a stove, I was able to study a plethora of framed press cuttings charting the road from tied house to 'people's pub'. The *Daily Mail* of 11 December, 1982, quotes one new shareholder, 69-year-old Harry Clark: 'I bought my first pint at the Red Lion for 4d (less than 2 pence) when I was fourteen. I didn't want to see the pub changed.'

You won't find an inn sign at this remote farmhouse, which is situated on a gravel drive in the South Downs. In fact, you won't find any sign at all. This is the Pub With No Name. It was the local of poet Edward Thomas (1878-1917) who was killed in the First World War, aged thirty-nine. His first poem, *Up in the Wind*, describes the pub he loved. The verses were inspired by a 'wild' young barmaid's feeling of isolation after returning from London in 1914:

…All I ever had to thank
The wind for was for blowing the sign down.
Time after time it blew down and I could sleep.
At last they fixed it, and it took a thief
To move it, and we've never had another:
It's lying at the bottom of our pond.

The poem offers one explanation for this 'nameless' pub. Whenever an inn sign has been put up it has been dismantled

*The pub that is so good it remains nameless. Even some of the beers are unnamed, at Hampshire's Pub with No Name.*

or stolen. The barman told me another: that locals had claimed there was a curse and, if the pub were ever properly named, bad luck would follow. Others say the moniker comes from a specially brewed strong ale called No Name. Folk started calling it 'The pub with No Name [bitter].' When I called, they were serving eight real ales, including Ringwood 49er, Bowman Wallops Wood, Fuller's London Pride and three with the No Name prefix (Best, Pale and Strong). Curiously, the barman said he was not at liberty to say who brews them. All the pump clips – including that for Fuller's London Pride – are anonymous, hand-written boards, making this the Pub With No Proper Pump Clips.

Most of the hostelry has a patina of antiquity, especially the two bars with their half-timbering, counter fronts forged from tree-trunk, old fireplaces and walls of bare stone and plaster. This style of décor, known as 'publican's rustic', was popular between the World Wars. Part of the quarry-tiled right-hand bar was once a shed and includes a corner devoted to Edward Thomas. Thankfully, a modern dining-room extension does not spoil things. But why is this pub set in a remote field? Dating from 1620, it was converted from a farmhouse, later becoming an inn with a smithy (now the lounge bar) servicing coaches and their passengers crossing the Downs. During the Napoleonic Wars, the highway was straightened, leaving the building isolated. Ergo, it has become the Pub With No Road. Outdoor seating, meals, real cider, adjacent camping. On CAMRA's Regional Inventory.

***White Horse*** (aka Pub With No Name), Monkey Lane, near Petersfield, GU32 1DA. Tel. 01420 588387. www.whitehorsepetersfield.co.uk

## ROBIN HOOD'S BAY, NORTH YORKSHIRE
### End of the road for Coast-to-Coast trekkers
### *Bay Hotel (formerly New Inn)*

*The Bay Hotel in Robin Hood's Bay represents journey's end for dozens of Coast to Coast walkers annually. A mule did the walk once and got a certificate from the bar.*

Clinging to a rock at the edge of the North Sea, the Bay Hotel displays a plaque that comes straight to the point: 'Coast to Coast Walk – 192 miles – THE END.' Many of the customers who stagger into the bar of this wave-lashed pub have completed one of the country's most gruelling, yet popular long-distance treks. To these battle-hardened celebrants, it is the ultimate pub and they are determined to sign the visitors' book, sink a pint or two and possibly purchase a special certificate bearing their name. Mostly, of course, they are people but on one notable occasion it was a mule. Author Hugh Thomson did the trek with a pack mule named Jethro, writing about it in a travelogue called *One Man and a Mule*, (Penguin Random House, 2017). Jethro was awarded his own certificate, before ritually dipping a hoof in the sea.

Over a pint of Theakston's Lightfoot Bitter, I chatted to a tall, tanned gentleman from Middlesbrough called Alby. He has walked the C-to-C, not once but fourteen times. 'It's not a walk in the park, it's equivalent to the ascent and descent of Mount Everest,' he asserted. It's also an international event, I discovered. Browsing the C-to-C visitors' book, I found it filled with names from Australia, the USA, Germany and many other countries. Alongside were comments like 'Best thing I've ever done – ever'; 'Did it in bits, now I'm in bits' and 'Wet, soggy and funny, to the end.'

There are views out to sea from the cosy bar, with its bench seating and real fire, and from the family room. There, you can access an outdoor terrace, grandly titled the Nautical North Sea Beer Garden. Exiting was bracing, as the wind was whipping up, creating white horses on the waves. Another bar downstairs, Wainwright's, named for Alfred W who devised the C-to-C in the 1970s, was closed. Four real ales were available, the others being Thwaite's Wainwright and Theakston's Bitter. Meals, accommodation, ambient music, dog friendly.

Nearby: One doesn't have to be a walker to enjoy Robin Hood's Bay. It is an unspoilt, picturesque fishing village nestling in a deep ravine. Other good pubs include Ye Dolphin and the Laurel Inn. The roads are narrow and steep, with all parking at the top of town. Regular buses from Whitby and Scarborough.

*Bay Hotel*, The Dock, YO22 4SJ.
Tel. 01947 880278.  www.bayhotel.info

## RYE, EAST SUSSEX
### A soup kitchen for the poor
### *Waterworks*

This diminutive, brick and timber building became the area's first micro-pub in 2018, having enjoyed a chequered history. It was first a pump-house, then a soup kitchen, public toilet and antique shop. The structure dates from 1718. Its role as municipal soup kitchen began in 1895, when the Guardians of the Rye Poor Law Union

*These circular brick recesses in the Rye Waterworks Micropub once contained vats of hot soup for the town's poor but now provide additional seating. All the furniture on the premises is for sale.*

enlarged it to incorporate two circular brick recesses. These, converted into seating but still recognisable, once contained huge, 70-gallon copper vats for soup, heated by coal fires. In 1907, the kitchen opened twice a week and tickets were distributed to the unemployed, and other deserving poor, at the Town Hall. Spoons four feet long were used to stir the steaming broths of vegetable, meat and bone and, at the appointed hour

…the odour of soup permeated the streets, from which came, scurrying and running, small boys and girls, carrying such handy receptacles as ewers, water cans, pots, basins, buckets and other articles… (Kenneth Clark, *Rye's Own Magazine*, May 2008)

Today, it is local real ale and cider, rather than soup that attracts visitors. A blackboard is updated with the daily offer: eight ales, including examples from Old Dairy, Romney Marsh, Hopfuzz and Filo when I visited; as well as ciders from Henderson, Nightingale and Norman Hunt. Beers are served direct from casks racked in a cooled cabinet, with future ones kept in the former coal cellar.

Another enticing feature is that the Waterworks continues one former role, i.e. as an antique shop, though with a difference. If customers like the table or chair they're using, or any other item of furniture, they are allowed to buy it. Also, the toilets are flushed by operating beer hand-pulls. A friendly pub, without ambient music; conversation is encouraged. Bar snacks, traditional games, dog friendly, outside seating.

Nearby: The historic Mermaid Inn was base for a notorious gang of smugglers.

**Rye Waterworks**, Tower Street, TN31 7AT. Tel. 01797 224110.  www.ryewaterworks.co.uk

## SAFFRON WALDEN, ESSEX
### The head of police murdered
### *Eight Bells*

It was All Hallows' Eve, 1849, when fifty-three-year-old William Campling, Chief Constable of Saffron Walden Borough Police, bade goodnight to the landlord. A few moments later, he lay badly injured in the doorway of his own house, both legs peppered with gunshot. He had left the pub just after 10pm with his friend William Brand, to make the 40-yard walk to his Bridge Street home. His assailant, it seems, was lying in wait beside the bridge over Madgate Slade (a stream). Brand wished Campling a good night and, a minute or so later, heard a bang and the cry 'I'm shot, I'm shot!' Surgeon Thomas Brown was summoned and helped carry the victim upstairs. Next morning, the surgeon extracted eight pieces of shot from his right leg and two from the left. Despite receiving rapid medical attention, Campling developed gangrene and died on 9 November.

A twenty-one-year-old man, Benjamin Pettit, was charged with his murder but found not guilty, despite Campling accusing him from his deathbed. No-one else was charged. The first murder of a serving Essex police officer is a crime that remains unsolved to this day. A commemorative plaque on the Slade bridge, just yards from the Eight Bells where the officer made his ultimate call, is a permanent reminder of this sad event. More details are on Essex Police Memorial Trust's Roll of Honour.

Now respected as a gastro-pub, it is equally welcoming if you just fancy a pint. It's a Grade II* listed, timber-framed gem in a town full of ancient buildings. Once a wool merchant's house, the structure dates from the fifteenth century. The oldest part is at right-angles to the road and is set out as an atmospheric dining hall, lined with sturdy beams soaring to a vaulted ceiling. The front section, where the bar counter occupies a corner, is furnished with armchairs, sofas and settles, while a fire blazes near the door. I enjoyed a Woodforde's Wherry (ABV 3.8%) but could have

chosen St Austell Brewery's Tribute or Sharp's Doom Bar, or wine from an extensive list.

Nearby: A stroll around town reveals two inns boasting remarkable architecture. The Cross Keys (reputedly haunted) was used as a base by Oliver Cromwell, while the Old Sun Inn (no longer a pub) is notable for its pargetting – decorative exterior plasterwork, including depictions of two figures. They are thought to be Tom Hickathrift and the Wisbech Giant, characters from East Anglian legend. Also, try navigating the largest turf maze in Europe, on the town's common (probably best attempted before drinking).

**Eight Bells**, 18 Bridge Street, CB10 1BU. 01799 522790. www.theeightbellssaffronwalden.com

*The timber-framed Eight Bells in Saffron Walden was a wool merchant's house in the fifteenth century. It is now a gastropub serving three real ales.*

*Plaque adjacent to the Eight Bells, marking the place where the town's High Constable was fatally shot in 1849.*

## SALISBURY, WILTSHIRE
### A mummified hand
### *Haunch of Venison*

*Salisbury's Haunch of Venison is six hundred years old and is known for its 'mummified hand'. Its owner was reputedly caught cheating at a game of cards.*

If buildings could talk, this peculiar old pub – with its juxtaposition of rooms, wood-panelled walls, creaking floors and steep, twisting staircase – would tell a hundred tales. Standing opposite the medieval Poultry Cross, around which live geese and hens were once traded, and overlooking the graveyard of St Thomas's church, this former church house inn has stood for more than six hundred years. Its interior dates from the fifteenth century (the most recent of subsequent alterations were around 1910). The bar counter has a rare pewter top and this is one of the few remaining hostelries with brass spirit taps for gin and fortified wine. Beer dispense is unconventional, too, the hand-pulls being positioned on the bar back and to one side. I ordered a pint of crisp, fruity Hop Back GFB (ABV 3.5%) and sat with several locals in the public bar, which they call the House of Commons. Then I adjourned to a cosy, cave-like inner sanctum (the House of Lords), where a 'mummified hand' and some faded playing cards are displayed in a fireplace bread oven.

The gruesome exhibit belonged to a customer, supposedly caught cheating at cards. It was found by workmen during the above renovation. I place the object in quotes as the barman didn't deny my observation that the hand is a replica. The 'real' hand has been stolen twice, once in 2004 – by pranksters who returned it six weeks later – and again in 2010 ('Severed hand of gambler stolen from pub,' *Daily Telegraph*, 16 March, 2010). He told me it is now in Salisbury Museum but the staff there denied any knowledge. 'We have whole skeletons here, why would we want a hand?' said a rather serious attendant. According to the *Telegraph* article, local legend says the hand's original owner is responsible for the pub being haunted. Richard Jones, author of *Haunted Britain and Ireland* (p.29, New Holland, 2001), states that ghostly footsteps have been heard pacing the upstairs rooms (now used by diners) between

*A dead man's hand? This item is on display in an old bread oven at the Haunch of Venison, in a room called the House of Lords.*

11.30pm and midnight. He also mentions a lady in a brilliant white shawl seen gazing from an upstairs window. As I read this, the neighbouring church clock daintily chimed the hour and the House of Commons, which had been animated, fell strangely quiet.

Other beers available were Hop Back Summer Lightning, Exmoor Ales Fox and Courage Best; also a wide choice of whiskies. On CAMRA's National Inventory. Meals, ambient music, dog friendly.

***Haunch of Venison***, 1 Minster Street, SP1 1TB.
Tel. 01722 411313. http://haunchpub.co.uk

## SANTON BRIDGE, CUMBRIA

### The world's biggest liar

### *Bridge Inn*

*Mike Naylor, aka Monkey Liar, holds his 'World's Biggest Liar Competition' trophy at the Bridge Inn, Santon Bridge, in 2018.*

Situated a stone's throw from England's highest mountain, amid the grandeur of the Lake District National Park, for much of the year this old coaching inn hosts hikers, climbers and tourists. Each November, however, it attracts ramblers of a different kind: talkative, extrovert types who enjoy telling tall stories. A slate plaque announces 'Home of The World's Biggest Liar Competition'. Far from being a new-fangled publicity stunt, it was a tradition that started in the late nineteenth century, under the tutelage of Will Ritson (1808-90). A publican from nearby Wasdale Head, Will was a natural storyteller. Customers were enthralled by his tales, including one where local turnips grew so large that villagers carved them out and used them as cowsheds.

The rules are straightforward – lawyers and politicians are barred as they are naturally 'economical with the truth' – but, otherwise, anyone can have a go at telling the most convoluted lie they can. There was a sense of jovial anticipation as the audience of about a hundred enjoyed a tattie pot supper and a Jennings ale or two. Then the entrants' stories began, including one about HRH Prince Charles swimming the Solway Firth in a kilt; another about a mine being opened on the Langdale Pikes, to excavate dark matter. The winner, an effervescent Mike Naylor, aka 'Monkey Liar' – a previous trophy holder – span a tale recalling his wondrous ride on the Hadron Collider and a trip up Mount Eiger on a Segway, wearing a magic tie. The punchline featured the words 'tie of the Eiger'. His £250 prize was donated to a local hospice. The sell-out evening (£12 including supper) was hosted by a compere. Part of its charm is that it's an all-amateur affair, attracting locals as well as tourists from as far as New Zealand.

The inn, a local CAMRA award winner, has a number of public rooms but its heart is a wood-beamed, bare-boards bar, with a mixture of upholstered bench seating, spindle-back chairs and stools. The range of ales was pleasing. It included Zenith and Sunset from Cross Bay (based in Morecambe), Wainwright Golden and several Jennings beers, notably their dark, warming Sneck Lifter (ABV 5.1%). After a pint of that, I felt almost brave enough to get on stage myself. Meals, accommodation, garden, dog friendly.

***Bridge Inn***, near Holmrook, CA19 1UX.
Tel. 019467 26221. www.santonbridgeinn.com

## SEASALTER, KENT
### A WWII battle on British soil
### *Sportsman Inn*

When two RAF Spitfires took on a Luftwaffe bomber over the Thames Estuary during the Battle of Britain in September 1940, it was an everyday occurrence. Successfully disabled, the Junkers Ju88 crash landed on the East Kent marshes, near Seasalter. A unit of 1st Battalion London Irish Rifles, billeted at this coastal pub, rushed to the scene. Instead of surrendering, the four-strong enemy aircrew engaged the soldiers, using the aircraft's machine guns. They had been ordered not to let the 'plane – with the latest

*Plaque at the Sportsman Inn, Seasalter commemorating the seventieth anniversary of the Battle of Graveney Marsh, in World War Two. A battalion of the London Irish Rifles was billeted at the pub when they were called to action.*

*The Kent marshes and estuary at Seasalter, near the spot where a Luftwaffe bomber crash landed. The Sportsman Inn is the whitewashed building in the distance (right-hand side).*

equipment – fall into enemy hands. A short but heavy exchange of fire ensued, in which one crewman was wounded. This became known as the Battle of Graveney Marsh, reputedly the last ground engagement fought on the British mainland (*Mail Online*, 21 August, 2010). The London Irish commander, Cpt. John Cantopher, then found an explosive demolition charge on the aircraft. He quickly removed it, throwing it into a ditch and got a George Medal for his bravery. According to reports, the British soldiers then supped pints of beer with their captives at the Sportsman before they were taken away. The aircraft was removed to Farnborough for examination.

These days, the Sportsman is better known as a gastro-pub than a military billet. A plaque commemorating the conflict was unveiled at the entrance by the London Irish Regimental Association in 2010. The pub's cuisine, directed by chef Stephen Harris, is renowned (a string of culinary awards is displayed on the bar and the menu is chalked up). Booking is necessary to secure a meal, but drinkers are always welcome. This is, after all, a 'grotty boozer by the sea' to use Harris's modest phrase. My pint of Whitstable Bay Pale from Shepherd Neame (ABV 3.9%) was on fine form and the spacious surroundings most agreeable. A display of work, all for sale, by local artists decorated the walls. Apart from that, decoration is minimal: bare boards and fireplaces (awaiting their winter fuel); tables were set with flowers. At the rear is a garden full of home-grown vegetables; to the front, benches where you can drink to the sound of birdsong, which fills the 'wide-sky' marshes.

Nearby: Brent geese, wading birds, hen harriers and merlins are often spotted on the South Swale Nature Reserve. For walkers, the Saxon Shore Way path is adjacent.

*Sportsman*, Faversham Road, near Whitstable, CT5 4BP. Tel. 01227 273370. www.thesportsmanseasalter.co.uk

## SLAD, GLOUCESTERSHIRE
### Laurie Lee's local
### *Woolpack*

Novelist and poet Laurie Lee lived in this tranquil valley for much of his life, and this was his local. As he was growing up, the youngest of a family of eight, the village was a place that was 'still mainly feudal…and nothing moved faster than a horse,' to quote the introduction to his *Cider with Rosie* (Hogarth Press, 1959). Tree-fringed and perched precariously on the valley side, with the churchyard where he now rests opposite, the Woolpack is well used and comfortably well-worn. It seems imbued with Lee's spirit, though this is no morbid shrine, rather the beating heart of the village. Copies of his books are displayed in the snug, along with photos and press clippings. They include an obituary for the real-life 'Rosie': namely Laurie's cousin Rosalind Buckland, who died in 2014, a few days short of her hundredth birthday.

The Woolpack in Slad was writer Laurie Lee's favourite pub and is little changed.

The stone-built pub is small but lengthy, with wooden floors, ageing settles, wild flowers displayed in bottles – and a piano for impromptu music sessions. Though divided into separate 'rooms', most customers, who seemed to be regulars, had gravitated to the busy 'inner sanctum', namely the bar. Others sat outside on benches, with a family playing cards on a vine-fringed terrace overlooking the valley. I was spoiled for choice ale-wise, with a tempting line-up, plus ample local cider. I plumped for the fruity Uley Bitter (ABV 4%). Other brews from Uley included Old Spot and Pig's Ear, with Clavell & Hind's Rookwood and Budding Pale from Stroud Brewery also on sale. No wonder Laurie felt at home in this, his regular haunt. As you'd expect, there was a seat with his name on it. He is buried in the graveyard opposite. Meals served, dog friendly, real fire. Nearby: Walk the Laurie Lee Wildlife Way – a map is affixed outside the pub.

*Woolpack*, GL6 7QA. Tel. 01452 813429. http://thewoolpackslad.com

## SOUTHAMPTON, HAMPSHIRE (1)
### A jail for POWs and cradle of aircraft construction
### *Dancing Man (aka the Wool House)*

A cavernous stone building dating from the twelfth century, this has only been a brewpub since 2015. That's when the Dancing Man Brewery transferred its kit from the nearby Platform Tavern. Following a French raid in 1338, the building was made into a secure warehouse for wool awaiting export. Throughout the eighteenth century, it served as a jail for Napoleonic prisoners of war (some of their names are carved in the roof beams). From 1908, it was home to Moonbeam Engineering, a boat building company owned by the family of pioneer aviator Squadron Leader Edwin Moon DSO. Inspired by the Wright Brothers, Moon produced early experimental aircraft. Most successful was a monoplane, Moonbeam II, which took to the skies two years later – from a

*Edwin Moon DSO with Moonbeam II, his second aircraft built in the Wool House, around 1910.*

farm that would become Southampton Airport. Among the building's more recent uses was as the city's Maritime Museum, housing *Titanic* relics. Brewery equipment is in full view, as are the medieval stone walls and their supporting timbers. Upstairs, a magnificent fourteenth-century arched roof, braced with Spanish chestnut, can be seen. This first-floor area is a restaurant, with a dedicated bar. There's lots of memorabilia, notably a timber jib crane that once stood in Shed 22 of the Eastern Docks; also historical local photos and a gallery of CAMRA awards (for the beers). I found the ales very moreish, and their names evocative, i.e. Bloody Red Baron, Sea City Gold, Big Casino and Big Bad Stout. Outside seating, dog friendly, occasional live music. A Grade I listed building.

***Dancing Man (Wool House)*, Town Quay, SO14 2AR. Tel. 023 8083 6666. www.dancingmanbrewery.co.uk**

*Southampton's medieval Wool House served as a prison for POWs, a maritime museum and an aircraft factory. It is now home to the Dancing Man brewery.*

## SOUTHAMPTON (2)
### Brothers who missed the *Titanic*
### *Grapes*

An ornate 'Grapes' sign above the entrance, embellished with a portrait of RMS *Titanic*, dates from the era of the great liners. Close to the docks, the pub was popular with ship crews and a plaque tells a remarkable story. Five of the crew of *Titanic* – namely three siblings, Alfred, Tom and Bert Slade and firemen John Podesta and William Nutbean – were drinking here shortly before

*The Grapes, Southampton, where five of the RMS* Titanic's *crew drank shortly before she sailed. A portrait of the ill-fated liner adorns the frontage.*

her maiden voyage in 1912. They left with just minutes to spare and, needing to cross railway tracks, their passage was interrupted by a passing train. Podesta and Nutbean dashed ahead and caught the ship in time. The three brothers waited for the train to pass, resulting in boarding being denied, as they were so late. The vessel left without them, sailing to its dreadful fate. Of 720 crew members with a Southampton address, more than 540 perished. Remarkably, both Podesta and Nutbean survived, however.

I enjoyed a pint of Grapes Ale (ABV 3.7%), brewed on the Isle of Wight, as I examined the pub's White Star and docks memorabilia, notably a large facsimile of a *Titanic* blueprint. Other ales were from Goddards, Wadworth and Sharp's. The two-bar pub has a period feel, not unlike the smoking room of an Edwardian liner, being full of polished dark wood, with etched glass windows and ornate mirrors completing the scene. Furnishings include high-back armchairs and sofas. Outside seating, ambient music.

Nearby: The pub features on the *Oxford Street Titanic Heritage Trail* leaflet. Sea City Museum in the Civic Centre has a permanent *Titanic* exhibition.

**Grapes**, 41-43 Oxford Street, SO14 3DP. Tel. 023 8033 3220.
www.thegrapessouthampton.co.uk

## SOUTHAMPTON (3)
### A Shakespearean trial
### *Red Lion*

Pub historian Ted Bruning calls this 'one of the treasures of our surviving medieval inns' *(David & Charles Book of Historic English Inns)*. Entering through the mock-Tudor frontage (rebuilt this way after wartime bomb damage) I found this late medieval hall-house breathtaking. A fourteenth-century, galleried Great Hall remains intact, including its substantial timber beams rising to the roof.

*A medieval great hall is the imposing heart of Southampton's Red Lion. A landmark trial, featured in Shakespeare's* Henry V, *was reputedly held there.*

The rear of the hall features a Tudor stone fireplace, with three suits of armour resting upon it. There are also the remains of an Elizabethan militia flag, looking very fragile behind its glass frame.

Known as the Court Room, it is claimed that in 1415 this was the scene of a trial – and the condemnation by Henry V – of two noblemen and a commoner who had planned to assassinate the king and his brothers. (Around the walls are the arms of Henry's fellow judges.) Known as the Southampton Plot, it features in William Shakespeare's *Henry V* (Act II, Scene 2). However, in his *Southampton in 50 Buildings* (Amberley, 2016) Garth Groombridge disputes the location, arguing that the hall wasn't built until the late fifteenth century and the trial is more likely to have been held in the castle.

Whether or not the story is true, I sensed the Red Lion was imbued with legend: my feelings were enhanced by a jug of Itchen Valley Hampshire Rose (ABV 4.2%). Hop Back Crop Circle (4.2%) and Weston's Rosie's Pig Cider were on handpump. An elderly parrot named Molly was in residence and I'm sure she could recite a tale or two. On CAMRA's National Inventory. Meals, real fires, ambient music.

**Red Lion**, 55 High Street, SO14 2NS. Tel. 023 8033 3595. http://theredlion.restaurantwebx.com

## SOUTH QUEENSFERRY, WEST LOTHIAN
### Setting for R.L. Stevenson's *Kidnapped*
### *Hawes Inn*

In my mind's eye I pictured the wrinkled ship's captain seated by the fire in this flagstone-floored, former coaching inn. He's a character in Robert Louis Stevenson's novel *Kidnapped*, as many a child knows. Though changed considerably since the author immortalized it, the hostelry once called Newhalls Inn retains some charm. It is worth visiting simply for its superb setting beside the Firth of Forth, in the shadow of the iconic Forth Bridge. I was

*The Hawes Inn, South Queensferry was a location visited by R.L. Stevenson and used in his novel* Kidnapped. *The Forth Bridge towers above.*

told Stevenson wrote part of the book there, staying in room 13 (page 6). The guest ale (Inveralmond's Lia Fail, ABV 4.7%) was suitably warming, as I'd entered with a shiver, while a brisk easterly gusted off the North Sea. (Other ales were from Caledonian and Sharp's.) A framed plan of the original Forth Bridge – designed but never built, as it was the work of the ill-fated Tay Bridge's architect – is an interesting feature. Meals, accommodation, dog friendly, garden.

Nearby: If you visit in August, look out for a character from folklore, the Burryman. He is covered in green burrs (sticky burdock seed heads) and led around town via all the pubs. Inside, he is fed whisky through a straw: a pub crawl with a difference.

**Hawes Inn**, 7 Newhalls Road, EH30 9TA. Tel. 0131 331 1990. www.vintageinn.co.uk

## STEVENTON, OXFORDSHIRE

### A dramatic entrance

### *North Star*

Customers reportedly enjoying a midnight lock-in at this village pub had their New Year's Eve, 2002 get-together dramatically curtailed when a man deliberately drove a mechanical digger into the walls. The culprit was none other than the owner, who was 'returning to the pub in a JCB from his nearby farm and "went bananas" at being refused a late-night drink' ('Landlord calls time…with JCB', the *Guardian*, January 3, 2003). 'The digger returned several times to crash into the pub like a battering ram,' adds the report. Part of the roof collapsed, though no one was injured. The pub, dating from the sixteenth century and listed on CAMRA's National Inventory, reopened several months later, following a £70,000 restoration.

When I first visited in 2001, long-time landlady Peggy Cox (then aged seventy-nine) was in charge, serving from a kitchen-cum-

*The North Star, Steventon in 2001, showing landlady Peggy Cox playing dominoes with the regulars. Peggy retired the following year, aged seventy-nine, by which time the pub had been in the Cox family for more than 175 years.*

servery stacked high with boxes of crisps, chocolate and crates of ale. She retired soon after my visit, by which time the pub had been run by the Cox family for 177 years. As I was pleased to see recently, it remains a classic. There's still no proper bar – customers are served from this ground floor 'cellar', via a stable door, a hatch in the lounge or, for garden customers, through the kitchen window. Walls of the public bar are panelled, with quarry tiled floors. At its heart is an enclosed wood-framed snug, set with time-worn settles facing a brick fireplace. Upper curtains would once have given drinkers greater privacy. Ales are locally sourced and served from the cask. I savoured a wholesome West Berkshire Good Old Boy, with other choices being Butts Organic Jester and Loose Cannon Bombshell, as well as real cider in summer. Toilets are outside, along with a wooden porch with bench seating. The garden features Aunt Sally pitches and an old GWR signal. Why a signal? The pub, which takes its name from a broad gauge engine introduced in 1838, was once regularly used by railwaymen. (The former station was favoured by I.K. Brunel for meetings, as it lay halfway between London and Bristol.) Quiet pub, dog friendly, traditional games.

Nearby: More GWR engines and memorabilia are displayed at Didcot Railway Centre.

*North Star*, 2 Stocks Lane, near Abingdon, OX13 6SG.

## STIPERSTONES, SHROPSHIRE

### The Devil's Chair Dawdle

### *Stiperstones Inn*

I visited this free house, a community hub tucked below the 6-mile Stiperstones ridge in the Shropshire Hills, as landlords Lara and Phil were preparing to celebrate the fiftieth anniversary of their family's ownership. The local 'knit and natter' knitting group was busy in one of the two bars. 'Come on in, we won't bite!' joked one woman. The inn is, however, better known for something a lot more energetic, and staged each Boxing Day for the last forty years. The Devil's Chair Dawdle or Dash is a 3-mile run over the moors of the surrounding national nature reserve, established by and starting from the inn. Hundreds of fell runners, some dressed as ballerinas, twin-headed ogres, pixies or Santas, attempt the feat – whatever the weather. 'We have raced in sunshine, rain, deep mud and thick snow but it's never cancelled,' the organizer told the *Guardian* (23 December, 2017). There are inducements to reach the peak: 'Supporters from the Shropshire Mining Club encourage weary souls with a drop of the hard stuff at the summit. They're getting on a bit, but take a couple of cases of whisky up,' he added.

The family also tend retired racehorses and were looking after Bevier, a descendant of the well-known thoroughbred Arkle, when I visited. The inn, established by 1850, is known for its wild whinberry (collected locally) infused gin, jam and ice-cream. The latter is used in desserts in the restaurant at the rear, part of which resembles a baronial hall. Rustic and cosy, with real fires, beams,

*The Stiperstones Inn, in the Shropshire Hills, is unofficial headquarters of the Devil's Chair Dawdle. Runners who reach the summit are rewarded with a tot of whisky. The pub is also known for its whinberry-infused gin.*

upholstered bench seating, the bar is decorated with horse brasses. Three ales were on offer: Six Bells' Mysterious Dark Mild from nearby Bishop's Castle (q.v.), Stonehouse Station Bitter and Wye Valley HPA, plus real cider. 'This is a great community pub, thanks to the licensees,' said the knitting circle woman. Praise indeed. Meals, accommodation, garden, dog friendly, darts. On CAMRA's Regional Inventory.

Nearby: There's a small village shop next-door, previously run by the pub. For walkers, there's the Shropshire Way.

***Stiperstones Inn***, near Minsterley, SY5 0LZ. Tel. 01743 791327.  www.stiperstonesinn.co.uk

## STIRLING, STIRLING & FALKIRK (1)
### The left-handed beer glass
### *Nicky-Tams Bar & Bothy*

Being sinister handed, I am always on the lookout for items designed for similar 'right-brained' individuals. Imagine my excitement when I heard that this establishment had announced, through its Facebook page

Volunteers required to try a new innovation, left-handed glassware. Please be early to claim your free pint, as limited availability.

The hapless individuals who turned up to test this glassware and claim their complimentary drink soon realised they had been victims of an April Fool's joke. The event was dated 1 April, 2014. The stunt is fondly recalled, however and the barman grinned when I asked if my pint of Caledonian 80/- could be served in a left-handed glass. 'We tried to use those glasses but couldn't get a handle on them,' he joked. A sense of humour permeates the pub, which bears the family crest of the original owner, Laird Graigengelt, above the front door. There are various amusing signs, one positioned beside the door so to be read when leaving:

*A handy bar: Nicky-Tam's Bar and Bothy is known for its sense of humour. Staff once told left-handed customers they could claim a free pint in a glass made specially for them.*

### A stopover for Prince Charlie's troops
### *Settle Inn (formerly Red Lion Inn)*

Nestling beneath the ramparts of Stirling Castle, this atmospheric, stone-built hostelry, which dates from 1733 (see the builder's mark outside) is the town's oldest pub. Its moment of fame came the following decade. In 1746, Bonnie Prince Charlie's troops commandeered the place while laying siege to the castle, during the Jacobite rising that ended disastrously at the Battle of Culloden. A vaulted room at the rear was originally a stable, according to the landlord, so the soldiers may have had to share shelter with their horses. On a foggy winter's afternoon, I found the place warm, welcoming and friendly, with a coal stove blazing. There's a low, beamed ceiling, wooden settles and a spacious bar counter, offering tempting delights. Cromarty Whiteout IPA (ABV 3.8%) and the same Highland brewer's Happy Chappy (4.2%),

'You are now entering grim reality.' Situated on the main street leading to the castle, Nicky-Tams is decorated with oddments, including a collection of tea-pots. Free-standing stoves, rough stone walls and a flagstone floor combine to create a time-worn atmosphere. As I was leaving, a customer told me he had once spotted a ghost on the stairs. (Haunted buildings feature strongly in the town's tourist offer, both this and the Settle Inn featuring on the Stirling Ghost Walk.) Meals, ambient music, regular live music in the upstairs function room. Selection of whiskies.

*Nicky-Tams*, 29 Baker Street, FK8 1BJ. Tel. 01786 472194.
www.nickytams.com

*Stirling's stone-built Settle Inn was commandeered by Jacobite troops laying siege to the castle above.*

plus Wadworth's 6X, were available, with a guest malt whisky and guest rum advertised. Some bearded musicians arrived shortly after me – live music, including a weekly folk session, is a popular feature. A finalist for the local CAMRA's Pub of the Year (2017). Dog friendly.

**Settle Inn**, 91 St Marys Wynd, FK8 1BU. Tel. 01786 463403.

## SWEFFLING, SUFFOLK
### The pub that rose from the dead
### *Sweffling White Horse*

Numerous CAMRA awards adorn the walls of this two-room village pub, which is friendly, quirky and prized by the locals. Yet it lay empty, unloved and boarded up for years, facing the threat of conversion to residential use, like many others. In 2011, it was rescued and revived by a couple with no experience of the pub trade and, initially, no interest either. Marie and Mark were office workers in Essex whose dream was to run an eco-friendly campsite. They set that up, complete with a yurt and gypsy caravan, on a leafy site at the rear. Their intention was simply to live in the former pub but 'after a couple of hours talking and many cups of tea' they agreed that they would revive the pub. As the previous owners had removed everything – including the bar – they were in no doubt about the challenge ahead.

Their belief in sustainable living has resulted in low voltage lighting – supplemented by candles – while heating is by wood-burner and range. There are bare brick walls, a quarry-tiled floor and this is a rare pub without a bar counter. The couple found they couldn't squeeze one in alongside a billiard table, piano and darts area. Instead, beers are drawn from the cask in a small tap-room. There were three micro-brewery ales and one local cider, plus a wide range of bottled ciders. I chose between Miss Behavin', a strong, black IPA (ABV 6.7%) from Station 1-1-9, and Reedcutter from Humpty Dumpty (4.4%) but opted for Moongazer Pacific Pale (3.9%),

*The Sweffling White Horse has no bar counter: beer is delivered to customers via the tap room door on the left. The pub specializes in microbrewery ales and locally sourced snacks.*

hoppy with a malty finish. Furnishings, collected from auctions and boot sales, include sofas, settles and old wooden chairs. Traditional games are a feature, as is music, with regular live sessions, morris dancing and an occasional mummer's play. It's mainly a pub for conversation: I found strangers don't remain so for long.

A device mounted by the door is a clocking-in machine, as once used in factories. The regulars have their own cards, which they can punch with arrival time. A homemade sign quotes author Roald Dahl: 'If you are interested in something…embrace it with both arms, hug it, love it and, above all, become passionate about it.' 'We've embraced the White Horse,' says Marie. 'We love it to bits.' Small beer garden, camping, self-catering cottage. Opening times are limited. Locally sourced snacks, dog friendly.

**The Sweffling White Horse**, Low Road (B1119), near Saxmundham, Suffolk, IP17 2BB. Tel. 01728 664178.
http://swefflingwhitehorse.co.uk

## TETBURY, GLOUCESTERSHIRE

### A message in a coffin

### *Trouble House*

A rare, if not unique, pub to have a railway platform specially built for its customers, Trouble House Halt was opened in 1959. Served (in its final years) by a diminutive, four-wheel railcar, it was closed just five years later, in the infamous Beeching cuts. Its name featured in Flanders and Swann's song *The Slow Train*, among a mournful list of closed stations. The last steam-hauled train ran in 1959, filled with rail enthusiasts. On the return journey, it wasn't meant to call but someone pulled the communication cord. The mutinous passengers then adjourned to the pub for a swift pint, before an urgent toot from the engine's whistle summoned them back. When the last scheduled train of all called in 1964, a coffin scrawled with scathing comments and filled with empty whisky bottles was loaded by 'mourners' in bowler hats. This unconventional petition was delivered to British Railways chairman, Dr Beeching, in London.

How did the pub's unique name come about? It has certainly seen its share of problems: built in the 1750s as the Waggon and Horses, it was on land known as The Troubles, due to its tendency to flood. Also, several of an early landlord's wives died young; another suffered financially when male customers were abducted by the Navy press gang. Business deteriorated further during agricultural riots in the 1830s. A mob set fire to a new haymaking machine hidden in a wagon, causing major damage to the building. Some claim that two landlords committed suicide. One became bankrupt and sadly hanged himself; the other drowned in a nearby pond. The building is reputedly haunted: the bar lady told me that she had glimpsed a 'blue lady' entering the kitchen. A barman, who lives upstairs, added that 'it is always spooky if you're alone here at night.'

Spectres aside, the place has no troubles now, being a popular spot for both diners and drinkers. It is well-known for cuisine

*There are various theories as to why the Trouble House is so-called but none of them deter customers, who come for its meals, homemade cake and Uley Bitter.*

using locally sourced ingredients; and homemade cake. It opens for breakfast and Sunday lunch is popular. I supped a pint of Uley Bitter (ABV 4%), the only draught ale, though there was a selection of bottled ones and Stowford Press cider. The stone-built hostelry is long, narrow and divided into a number of rooms, with distressed old beams, sagging ceilings, log fires and wooden and stone floors. A shady courtyard and lawn is complemented by an outdoor bar. Ambient music.

Nearby: The former railway line now provides a tree-fringed walk into town.

*Trouble House*, Cirencester Road (A433), GL8 8SG.
Tel. 01666 502206. www.thetroublehouse.co.uk

## WAREHAM, DORSET

### Following the Court Leet

### *Duke of Wellington*

Over four evenings in late November, Wareham hosts a pub crawl with a difference. It has taken place since medieval times and involves a group of strangely dressed men carrying some equally strange accessories. They are officers of the Court Leet, upholders of a feudal system of justice once seen in many parts of the country. Wareham is one of the few places where these traditions continue. The court's official powers have long ceased,

*With much merriment, Aletasters of the Wareham Court Leet check the strength and quality of the beer in the Duke of Wellington. After trying it, they hand the ceremonial tankard round for others to sample.*

but the officers and judges carry out their duties diligently, with more than a touch of showmanship and a sharp sense of humour.

At each pub, the officials – led by a top-hatted supervisor called the Bailiff – are introduced to the landlord, who must abide by all instructions. A quart of ale is dispensed into a 200-year-old pewter pot and checked for measure, quality and strength by a pair of Aletasters. The beer is then passed around for sampling. Bread Weighers check the establishment's bread, using an ancient pair of scales, before the Carniter is presented with some meat or poultry, which he proceeds to cook on a portable stove before tasting. There is also a Leather Sealer checking the quality of the town's leather goods and two Constables in Victorian uniform, ensuring law and order is maintained (the proceedings can get lively). One of the more obscure tasks is examining the pub chimneys. Introduced after a major fire in 1762, it is carried out by the Surveyors of Chimneys and Mantles, using chimney-sweeps' poles and brushes. I also noticed a man wearing a fleece coat who, it turned out, was a Scavenger. His time-honoured duty was to check the lanes and privies of the town (in other words, a sanitation inspector). Two

pubs are inspected each night from Monday to Thursday (www. court-leet.org). On the Friday, the full court meets in the Town Hall at midday – when the clock strikes thirteen – and members of the public are welcome. I had a thoroughly enjoyable evening; the atmosphere in the pubs is jovial, with plenty of heckling. All the officers are volunteers who consider their roles to be an honour. In real life, jobs include mechanic, gas engineer and newsagent, though many are retired.

I have featured the Duke of Wellington since that was the focus for much of the evening I attended. Its ales included the malty, fruity Fossil Fuel (ABV 4.1%) from the Isle of Purbeck brewery, though I could have equally enjoyed Timothy Taylor Landlord, Titanic Plum Porter or Greene King Gangly Ghoul. Down the road at the thatched Kings Arms – home of the Purbeck Independent Simpleton's Society – they were serving the moreish Hog's Back TEA and two Black Sheep ales, while in the harbourside Old Granary it was Badger Bitter and others from Hall & Woodhouse. Feel confident that, wherever they go, those Court Leet officials are fine judges of a good pub. Accommodation.

***Duke of Wellington**, 7 East Street, BH20 4NN. Tel. 01929 553015. www.dukewareham.co.uk*

*Some of the officials of the Wareham Court Leet, who inspect each pub's premises, food and drink, led by a top-hatted Bailiff (second from left).*

## WELLINGBOROUGH, NORTHAMPTONSHIRE
### Railway 'ammo room' recalls train crash
### *Little R'Ale House*

Did you know that detonators are placed on railway tracks in emergencies, to warn approaching trains of obstructions on the line ahead? In the past, hundreds of these explosive gadgets were stored in this diminutive building on Wellingborough Station, lending it the nickname 'the ammo room'. In 2016, the Grade II listed structure was transformed into a popular micro-pub. Drinkers, who enjoy a range of ales and ciders out of all proportion to the pub's size, can inspect an opening hatch through which detonators were passed to railway staff. There are also historic railway photographs, some showing the aftermath of the Wellingborough railway crash of September, 1898. A Royal Mail

*The Little R'Ale House, on Wellingborough station, once housed explosives but is now peaceful, save for the hum of conversation and sound of ale being poured.*

trolley rolled off the adjacent platform, derailing a London to Manchester express: seven people were killed and dozens injured.

There are four regularly changing ales – from Potbelly, Elliswood, Framework and Blackpit on my visit – along with local draught ciders. This is a friendly place, so be warned, I got into some interesting banter with the locals and almost missed my train. Darts, dog friendly, outdoor seating.

*Little R'Ale House*, Wellingborough Station, Midland Road, NN8 1NA. Tel. 07711 928330. https://thelittleralehouse-bar.business.site

## WELWYN GARDEN CITY (NEAR), HERTFORDSHIRE
### A horse without a head
### *White Horse (formerly Chequers)*

The beauty of Burnham Green belies its grisly folk tale, recalled in the name of the house beer, Headless Horse. An adjacent sunken lane is said to be haunted by a white horse, which appears minus its head. In more superstitious times, locals were afraid to walk or ride along it. There are two historical explanations for the superstition. One is the lane follows an ancient boundary between rival Danelaw and Saxon lands – a white horse appeared on Danish battle flags of the period. The other is that, during the Civil War, a horse belonging to an executed Royalist, Farmer Pennyfather, was beheaded by Roundheads as it wouldn't leave its master. The Grade II listed property dates from the seventeenth century but has been much altered, having contemporary decor. Beers, including the house ale and various seasonal ones, are by McMullen's. Meals, garden (with duckpond), dog friendly, occasional live music.

*White Horse*, 1 White Horse Lane, Burnham Green, AL6 0HA. Tel. 01438 798100. www.whitehorseburnhamgreen.com

## WHITEHAVEN, CUMBRIA
### Where an invasion happened (almost)
### *The Vagabond*

We can thank pubs for many things but possibly their greatest achievement is scuppering an invasion of England. By the American navy, no less. It was led by John Paul Jones (1747-92) who was a Scot by birth and started his maritime career in Whitehaven, sailing at the age of thirteen. After a working life of mixed fortunes, employed on slave and merchant ships, he began anew in America. When the American War of Independence broke out, he joined the fledgling Continental Navy. In 1777, Jones set sail for Europe as captain of the newly commissioned USS *Ranger*. The following April, they snuck into the harbour at Whitehaven after dark. Leading two boats of fifteen men, he planned to set fire to the numerous British ships at anchor, spike the defensive guns ashore and light more fires in town. Unfortunately for him, the raiding party's lanterns ran out of fuel, so a party was ordered to a quayside beer house to seize some. The temptation to stop for a drink – and another – proved too much. Dawn was breaking by the time the drunken commandos staggered back to their comrades. The resulting fires were soon extinguished – only one of some two hundred ships was damaged. Jones and his fellows escaped successfully, however, as the British guns had been successfully sabotaged.

It appears the public house in question is long gone but the Vagabond is an appropriate one in which to contemplate this historic event. The street in which it stands is the one where locals raised the alarm, in the small hours of 23 April, 1778. It is in the Georgian harbour, with its cobbled streets and commemorative plaque, on the site of the Whitehaven Battery. This brass stands a few hundred yards from the pub door, beside a cannon with the statue of an American sailor 'spiking' it. The diminutive, though well-appointed hostelry serves a pleasing range of ales – from brewers including Ennerdale, Cumbrian, Keswick and Hawkshead. It was declared CAMRA (West Cumbria) Pub of the Season shortly before my 2018 visit. They do a good tot of rum, too: the town prospered on its import. Meals, dog friendly, occasional live music.

*The Vagabond*, 9 Marlborough Street, Off Strand Street, CA28 7LL. Tel. 01946 66653. www.thevagabondpub.co.uk

## WHITTLESEY, CAMBRIDGESHIRE
### Home of the Straw Bear
### *New Crown*

The sense of anticipation in this thatched hostelry, shortly before the arrival of the Straw Bear, was palpable. Men with feathers in their top hats repeatedly checked watches and women garlanded with flowers laughed nervously. Impatient children tugged at adults' coats, pleading 'is he here yet?' I was attending the Whittlesea (sic) Straw Bear Festival (www.strawbear.org.uk). Officially, this is a celebration of music and dance but, unofficially, a chance to have a damn good drink and a laugh in mid-January. An otherwise grim, grey time of year. I should add that this isn't a story about one pub, rather a whole coterie of them, in this ancient Fenland town. It seems to have more than the average number for its size. These establishments unite, with thousands of people, in celebration of a dumb thatched beast, the Straw Bear. Despite its name, the New Crown dates from the mid-seventeenth-century and is Grade II listed. A busy local, with oak beams, bare boards and a well-used dartboard, there are normally two real ales available. During the festival, this extends to eight, including Elgood's Straw Beer (ABV 4%), brewed specially for the event and drawn straight from the cask.

Since the early nineteenth century, it was a local custom to dress a man in straw and parade him around town in January (the weekend closest to Plough Monday). Straw Bear has always been something of a local celebrity. Led by a bowler-hatted Keeper, he would dance in exchange for beer, food or money. Farm hands

*The Straw Bear, accompanied by his Keeper and assorted followers, strides past the New Crown (background) on his rounds, during an annual festival in his name. The whole of Whittlesey comes alive for the occasion and several beers are brewed specially for it.*

supplemented their meagre income this way, during a lean period. The fun was stopped by police in 1909, being seen as a form of cadging. The custom was revived in 1980 and has been held ever since in aid of charity, growing into a festival of traditional dance and folk music. Morris and Molly dance teams – many with their faces blackened or otherwise disguised – along with longsword dancers and costumed figures, come from all over the country. Roads are closed for the main parades; performances take place outside pubs and in the market square. There's a carnival atmosphere. Most pubs stock extended beer and cider ranges and open additional bars to cope with demand. Meals, dog friendly.

**New Crown**, 58 High Causeway, PE7 1QA. Tel. 01733 205134. Festival website: www.strawbear.org.uk

## Some other Whittlesey pubs

***Black Bull Inn***. Stone-built, Grade II listed inn on the main street, serving six real ales during my visit. 18-20 Market Street, PE7 1BD. Tel. 01733 203314.

***Boat Inn***. A local with a loyal following, it has a boat-shaped bar counter and a petanque court. Good ale range, usually including one from Grainstore. 2 Ramsey Road, PE7 1DR. Tel. 01733 202488.

***George Hotel***. Inn dating from 1770, when named the George and Star. Now a J.D. Wetherspoon pub. It was serving no fewer than three specially brewed ales: Elgood's Straw Beer, Grainstore Straw Bear Festivale and Oakham Ales' Straw Bear Ale. 10 Market Place, PE7 1AB. Tel. 01733 359970.

***Letter B***. A community local and winner of multiple CAMRA awards, keeping a wide range of ales. It is something of an unofficial headquarters for organisers of the Straw Bear Festival, following closure of the Bricklayers Arms. There were at least 13 ales available during my visit on a festival Saturday, including examples from Tydd Steam, Lacons, Black Sheep and Tiny Rebel. 53-57 Church Street, PE7 1DE. Tel. 01733 206975.

## WIDECOMBE-IN-THE-MOOR, DEVON
### The chest with three locks
*Rugglestone Inn*

**Tom Pearse, Tom Pearse, lend me your grey mare,**
**All along, down along, out along, lee,**
**For I want for to go to Widecombe Fair…**

Sadly, Uncle Tom Cobley wasn't propping up the bar when I called. However, a set of Victorian prints illustrates Widecombe Fair – Tom and his mates' destination in the folk song. This rugged,

*Rain is a regular occurrence on Dartmoor but it doesn't stop customers visiting the Rugglestone Inn, where beer is served straight from the cask.*

stone-built pub stands on the edge of a handsome Dartmoor village. In the eighteenth century it was a farmhouse, only gaining a licence in the 1820s. That's because a nearby alehouse was burnt down. The guilty parties were said to be local women, tired of their husbands' proclivity for ale. In the days before the NHS and social security, the bar was home to Widecombe Sick Club, a well-organized community welfare society. Inhabitants subscribed to receive poor relief, medical treatment – even funding for funerals when in need. The cash was counted out over foaming pints of ale, the accounts being secreted in a wooden chest that still has pride of place. It had three locks, the keys to each being held by a different committee member. All had to attend before a meeting could start.

This is a peaceful, timeless place. The public bar floor is of concrete screed; tables and benches are rustic. A well-chosen

selection of beers is served direct from casks set on an old stillage. On my visit there was Rugglestone Moor Ale from Teignworthy, Dartmoor Brewery's Legend, Hanlon's Yellowhammer (very hoppy), Vog Speak Easy IPA, plus local cider. The landlord's pigs, ducks, turkeys and chickens are an alfresco attraction. On CAMRA's Regional Inventory; Alastair Sawday gave it an 'authentic pub' award. Meals served, garden, dog friendly, traditional games, real fire.

Nearby: The Tom Cobley Tavern at Spreyton (EX17 5AL) is where the eponymous Mr Cobley and chums (in the song Widecombe Fair) are reputed to have departed from in 1802, on a borrowed grey mare.

***Rugglestone Inn**, TQ13 7TF. Tel. 01364 621327.*
*www.rugglestoneinn.co.uk*

## WINCHESTER, HAMPSHIRE (1)
### An obsessive collector
### *Black Boy*

'We sat opposite a giraffe and box with squirrels playing snooker… there was a toilet seat, with a head popping out of it, on the ceiling.' One visitor's attempt, on the TripAdvisor website, to describe a sojourn at a pub that defies the written word. A museum-like display of memorabilia occupies every square foot of this neighbourhood local, near the River Itchen. It is the result of landlord David Nicholson's determination, since 1995, to scour auction houses and antique shops for the unusual, when he is not playing croquet. (I later learn he is rather good, playing barefoot and calling it 'outdoor snooker.')

Away from the city's tourist trail, a short riverside stroll took me to this real ale haven, a million miles away from being a chain pub. There were five locally brewed ales: I enjoyed a Saxon Bronze (ABV 3.8%) from the town's Alfred's Brewery. Others were from Flower Pots, Hop Back and Bowman, with real cider and gin also

*A model boat and 'plane, a stuffed baboon, pony and calf, assorted electrical equipment and numerous fire buckets adorn this corner of the Black Boy, Winchester.*

well represented. There is a jumble of rooms around the central servery, with flag-stoned and wood floors, and old beams. Some items are carefully 'categorized' – such as fire-buckets, blowlamps, smokers' pipes, spectacles and clocks. Others are displayed more randomly, particularly stuffed animals and model aircraft. Customers carry on conversations, oblivious to being seated next to a prosthetic leg or nest of giant wasps. Some books have been sawn off to fit three-inch shelves, adjacent to the toilet doors, fashioned from printers' blocks. Looking for the comfiest chairs? They're near the giraffe and camel's head. 'I wanted something for people to look at,' says David, the master of understatement. Meals, garden, dog friendly, real fires, occasional live music, accommodation.

**Black Boy**, 1 Wharf Hill, SO23 9NQ. Tel. 01962 861754.
www.theblackboypub.com

## WINCHESTER (2)
### A lady awaits her execution
### *Eclipse Inn*

It was a sombre day, in September 1685, when Lady Alicia Lisle stepped from an upstairs window, onto a scaffold that was hastily erected in the street outside. She knelt calmly, in front of an angry crowd, and was beheaded for the crime of sheltering traitors. They were three supporters of the Monmouth Rebellion. Unknown at the time to this frail lady in her late sixties, the three men were fleeing from defeat at the last battle fought on English soil, the Battle of Sedgemoor. Initially sentenced to burning to death by the infamous Judge Jeffreys, Alicia's sentence was commuted to beheading, on her appeal to James II. Her spirit, a grey shadow, reputedly haunts the hostelry where she was briefly imprisoned.

*The Eclipse Inn was used for the execution of Lady Alicia Lisle in 1685. Some believe she haunts the oak-beamed hostelry.*

Despite its mock Tudor façade, the building dates from 1540, when it was a church rectory, becoming an ale-house *circa* 1750. Small and pleasingly uncluttered, it is listed on CAMRA's Regional Inventory. An antique Strong's Brewery (Romsey) lantern graces the exterior. The oak-beamed front bar, with its polished wood counter and solid fuel stove, is cosy. Some seating is provided by well-worn settles and benches, with more outside on the pavement (blankets available). Customers were a mixture of locals and tourists: the cathedral is but a few paces. I started with a flavoursome 'BOB' ale from Wickwar (ABV 4%); other choices were Timothy Taylor's Landlord, Ringwood Razorback and Sharp's Doom Bar. I was later joined by members of my family, who enjoyed the sad tale of Lady Lisle, though no ghost was sensed, even after a few drinks. Meals, dog friendly, occasional live music.

**Eclipse Inn**, 25 The Square, SO23 9EX. Tel. 01962 865676. http://the-eclipse-winchester.co.uk

## WINDLESHAM, SURREY
### Peripatetic pram race pit-stop
### *Half Moon*

This is a delightful, peaceful pub in a bucolic Surrey village. Except on one day a year (Boxing Day), when everything goes a little crazy. The Windlesham Pram Race has been held each Christmas for the last fifty years. It is a pub crawl on an epic scale, with the Half Moon an important staging point. Teams dressed in a wide array of outfits, push (or ride) wheeled decorated objects – they can only loosely be described as prams – along a 3-mile course through the village, in aid of charity. It is a colourful, good humoured spectacle. Hundreds of spectators break off from their festive feasting to witness – on this occasion – 'Chas and Dave' impressionists wheeling a piano; a mobile *Saturday Night Fever* dancefloor; some 'Zombie Brides', complete with chainsaws; a Batmobile with appropriate Marvel characters and a pack dressed as 101 Dalmations accompanying their portable kennel,

*A pram disguised as the Batmobile, accompanied by 'Batman' and his cohorts, leave the Half Moon during the Windlesham Pram Race. The Boxing Day charity event attracts hundreds of competitors and supporters.*

to name a few. Crowds cheer the competitors and join the libations at no fewer than five pubs, of which the Half Moon was well prepared. Aside from the main bar it had set up two alfresco ones, including one reserved for participants, as well as a barbeque and hog-roast. The car park became a pram pit-stop, complete with portaloos. Roads are closed from 11am so everyone is able to mill about in safety, drop coins in myriad charity buckets (£9300 raised for local good causes in 2018) and pose for selfies with the fancy-dressed participants.

I hadn't enjoyed myself so much on Boxing Day since I was a child; the beer was rather good, too. I had a Flack Manor Flack's Double Drop (ABV 3.8%), while other choices included Hop Back Summer Lightning, Theakston's Old Peculiar, Fuller's London Pride and Hardy & Hanson's Rocking Rudolph, plus real cider. The former coaching inn is worth visiting at any time of year. I was told it has been in the same family for one hundred years; it has a genuine community feel and eight real ales are normally available. There are stone and wood floors, blazing stoves and a large rear garden and function room. Other events include classic car meets. Meals, dog friendly, ambient music.

**Half Moon**, Church Road, GU20 6BN. Tel. 01276 473329. thehalfmoonwindlesham.com   www.pramrace.com

## WISBECH, CAMBRIDGESHIRE
### A gamesman remembered
### *Rose Tavern (formerly Riverside Tavern)*

It was a surreal experience to walk into a pub where all eight customers were seated around the bar holding clenched fists. No, a fight was not about to start, I was witnessing one of the regular games of spoof\*, one of the community get-togethers for which this pub is known. A brass plaque beside the bar commemorates the man who started the tradition, some twenty years ago. Peter Charnley – 'friend, companion, gamesman' – died in 2001, aged seventy-five. A championship event is held in his honour each September, on Peter's death anniversary. Regular games are held at least weekly;

*Plaque to Peter Charnley (1926-2001), who started the tradition of 'spoof' in the Rose Tavern, Wisbech.*

everyone is welcome. They are occasions for light-hearted banter as well as fund-raising (coins go into a charity box). The rate of customers' quaffing was restrained, especially considering the delicious Piston Bob (ABV 4.6%) was on handpump. It hails from the nearby Tydd Steam Brewery whose brewer, Will Neaverson, also creates Beartown for the Whittlesea Straw Bear event (q.v.). Fuller's London Pride was also on; guest ales change often.

The Rose Tavern is a one-room, traditional pub, situated on one of England's most beautiful Georgian streets, beside the River Nene. There are no distractions such as television, ambient music or gaming machines, this being a place for conversation, traditional games, or simply enjoying a pint. Outside toilets, garden.

Nearby: The 200-year-old Elgood's Brewery, with its visitor centre, shop and garden, is a short walk away.

\*Spoof is a strategy game, often [played] in bars and pubs where the loser buys the other participants a round of drinks. In each round the objective is to guess the aggregate number of coins held in concealment by the players. Play proceeds clockwise around the circle until each player has ventured a guess regarding the total number of coins. (Wikipedia.)

**Rose Tavern**, 53 North Brink, PE13 1JX. Tel. 01945 588335.

*The Rose Tavern is an unspoilt, traditional pub on a Georgian thoroughfare in Wisbech.*

## WOOLPIT, SUFFOLK
### Village of the green children
### *Bull Inn*

'There are things that happen that people can't explain, aren't there?' The bar lady was referring to a coming 'psychic' event, led by a professional medium, in the pub. It was an apt statement in a village known for its folk tale of two 'alien' children. According to the medieval writers Ralph of Coggeshall and William of Newburgh, the mysterious brother and sister – who both bore a green complexion – appeared in Woolpit at harvest-time, in the twelfth century. They were of normal physical appearance, except for their skin colour. They wore unfamiliar clothes, spoke in an unknown language, and refused to eat anything other than raw beans. They eventually ate other food and lost their green pallor, according to the tale, but the boy was weak and soon died. His sister regained her health, was taught English and explained that they had come from St Martin's Land. It was a twilight world where the sun never shone, and whose inhabitants were green. They could not explain where their land was, nor how they had got from it to Woolpit. Though the story seems far-fetched, a wrought-iron village sign incorporates the young pair holding hands and the village church, St Mary's, displays a copperplate translation of William of Newburgh's description, published (in Latin) in 1618.

*The Bull Inn, Woolpit. Raw beans are rarely on the menu these days.*

*Woolpit's village sign depicts the mysterious green children who are said to have arrived in the seventeenth century.*

Though the Bull has no direct link with the story, it is a historic inn at the heart of the village. It has been given a contemporary makeover and extended to include a restaurant. There were three real ales: two from local brewer Adnams – Ghost Ship and Southwold Bitter – the other a guest, Humdinger from Joseph Holt (also a choice of bottled ciders and gins). A spacious garden, complete with a 'secret' wooded part, is reached through a picket gate. I sat on a bench with my ale, contemplating Woolpit's enduring mystery, in this serene spot. A case of aliens from a parallel world or ancient science fiction fable? I leave you to decide. Ambient music, occasional live music, darts, snooker, accommodation.

*Bull Inn*, The Street, near Bury St Edmunds, IP30 9SA. Tel. 01359 240393. www.bullinnwoolpit.co.uk

## WORCESTER, WORCESTERSHIRE
### The Merry Monarch's death-defying escape
### *King Charles II*

This timber-framed edifice is a Scheduled Ancient Monument, Grade II* listed and scene of an exciting event in English history. A plaque by the front door declares: 'From this house King Charles II escaped his enemies after the Battle of Worcester…' In 1651, after his defeat in the Civil War by Cromwell's army, Charles was on the run. The monarch had a price on his head and half the country would soon be after him. According to tradition, he briefly returned to these lodgings before escaping by the back door, as Roundhead soldiers battered down the front one. His dash to the south coast – and, ultimately, safety in France – involved a tortuous route, time spent hiding in an historic oak tree (many pubs are still called the Royal Oak as a reminder) and the support of followers who risked death to help. On his restoration to the throne, he became known as the Merry Monarch.

The building's two floors are a creaking blend of oak beams, panelled walls, sloping floors (particularly upstairs), with wooden benches and settles. It's hard to believe it suffered a major fire and was derelict for more than a decade. Much of the interior was sourced from other historic buildings. An impressive chimney-piece, for example, including a carving of three diners fleeing the devil, came from Sidbury House and has been dated to 1635. Originally part of a spacious wool merchant's residence built in 1577, now called King Charles House, the structure once continued around the street corner. Much was destroyed in an eighteenth-century fire and replaced by a separate Georgian building. It was restored in the mid-1960s, used as a museum and antique shop, then a restaurant, only becoming a pub around 2012. In the words of an amateur historian I met within: 'It's not the oldest pub in Worcester but it is the oldest building being used as one.' He then lifted a trap-door at the rear of the bar, revealing an *oubliette*, a circular void beneath the floor. 'Look at this. It has

*The plaque outside the King Charles II, which is a Scheduled Ancient Monument.*

been described as a well but may have been a dungeon; I'm sure it pre-dates the building.'

An assemblage of ten real ales, from Craddock's and associated breweries, is on hand-pull (I had the amber session ale, River Steam, ABV 3.8%). There are real ciders and, at the time of visiting, the menu specialized in pies. An atmospheric place, where the history is palpable and the beer eminently quaffable. Meals, traditional games, dog friendly, real fires.

Nearby: Those interested in the city's Civil War history should visit the Commandery, which was the Royalist headquarters.

*King Charles II*, 29 New Street, WR1 2DP.
Tel. 01905 726100. www.thekingcharleshouse.com

*King Charles II escaped from this house, now a pub of the same name, after his defeat at the Battle of Worcester. It is a rare outlet for Craddock's Ales of Stourbridge.*

*Detail of charred timbers on the Green Dragon's frontage, showing how narrow its escape was from the fire that virtually destroyed the town.*

## WYMONDHAM, NORFOLK
### The Great Fire survivor
### *Green Dragon Tavern*

One Sunday morning in 1615, a terrible fire raged through town. It seemed to start in two areas simultaneously, spread quickly and would destroy more than a quarter of the buildings. Most people were in church, so escaped with their lives. Somehow, the White Swan, as this half-timbered pub was then known, survived too – but only just. Close examination of the frontage reveals deep scorch marks on the timbers, resembling badly burnt toast. The blaze was attributed to arson and four people were hanged for the crime. Perhaps it was divine intervention that saved the hostelry? It is just a few hundred yards from Wymondham Abbey and a tunnel is supposed to have run from the cellar to this Benedictine priory (a locked door in the bar is intriguingly marked 'To the Abbey'!). The Grade II* building features a Tudor mantelpiece, with a curious carved head beneath; beams, wood panelling, leaded windows and built-in settles.

A wide range of events is held, including a twice-yearly beer festival that attracts visitors to a secluded garden and barn. There were four ales on my visit: Wolf Battle of Britain (ABV 3.9%), Dark Star Hophead (3.8%), Newby Wyke Black Squall (4.6%) and the house beer, Green Dragon from Marston's (3.6%). A CAMRA award winner. Real fires, dog friendly, occasional live music. On CAMRA's Regional Inventory.

***Green Dragon Tavern***, 6 Church Street, NR18 0PH. Tel. 01953 607907. www.greendragonnorfolk.com

*The Green Dragon not only survived the great fire of Wymondham in 1615 but is still a popular, and CAMRA award-winning, tavern.*

# 3. APPENDIX: ITINERARIES FOLLOWED BY THE AUTHOR

Many of the pubs featured in this book were visited during general tourist trips to cities and regions, or when meeting friends; on other occasions I made a specific trip to see one pub. Sometimes, I made up itineraries to see several hostelries over a longer period. I am sharing these for the interest of readers. I used a variety of means of transport, as described, but in all cases (except central London) you could easily substitute car travel. Locations in **bold** refer to pub entries in the Gazetteer starting on page 17. Where a bike is mentioned, I used a Brompton. This folding bicycle can be carried without restriction on trains and most buses. In most cases, other pubs were visited en route but these are excluded for clarity. These trips took me to some interesting places I probably wouldn't have visited without the incentive of the pubs.

**1.** Cumbria and the Lake District, by public transport and bike

Train to Brigg. Cycle to **Santon Bridge** (overnight). Cycle back to Brigg, train to **Whitehaven**, train to Workington, bus to **Keswick** (overnight). Bus to Ambleside, cycle to **Ambleside** – Barngates (Drunken Duck), cycle to **Near Sawrey**, cycle to Bowness on Windermere via ferry (overnight). Train home.

**2.** Shropshire and a bit of Herefordshire and Wales, by car

**Leintwardine, Bishop's Castle** (overnight). **Stiperstones, Atcham, Edgerley** (overnight, campsite). **Llanarmon Dyffryn Ceiriog** (overnight). **Marford**, then home.

**3.** The Peak District, by public transport and bike

Train to Cromford, bike to **Crich**, bike to **Bonsall**, bike to Cromford (overnight). Bus to Brierlow Bar (bookshop), bike to **Earl Sterndale**, bike to **Flash**, bike to Upper Hulme (overnight, bunk barn). Bus to Buxton, train home.

**4.** East Anglia, by car

**Norwich** (overnight). **Wymondham, Sweffling** (overnight), **Woolpit, Hempstead**, then home.

**5.** Scotland, by train and on foot

Train to **Dundee** (overnight). Train or bus to **Broughty Ferry**, return to Dundee, trains to **Perth**, **Stirling** and **Edinburgh** (overnight). Trains to **South Queensferry** and **Musselburgh** (overnight). Train back to Edinburgh, walk Innocent Railway Path (or bus) to **Duddingston** and back. Train home from Edinburgh.

**6.** Southern cities, by train

Train to **Winchester** and **Southampton** (overnight). Train to **Salisbury**, then home.

**7.** East and West Sussex, via South Downs, by car

**Lyminster, Ashurst**, Lewes (overnight). **Alfriston, East Dean, Hooe, Hastings** (overnight). **Rye**, then home.

**8.** London's river and Docklands, on foot

Underground to Canary Wharf in **Docklands**. Walk to the Ledger Building, continue to **Limehouse** (Grapes). Follow Thames Path to **Wapping** (Prospect of Whitby and Town of Ramsgate). Return from Wapping Overground station or continue along the riverside, via St Katharine's Dock, to Tower Hill Underground.

# BIBLIOGRAPHY

Ainsworth, Paul with Durbridge, Russ and Slaughter, Michael (Editors), *Real Heritage Pubs of the South West*, St Albans, CAMRA, 2019.

Alexander, Marc, *A Companion to the Folklore, Myths & Customs of Britain*, Sutton Publishing, 2002. (Reference for several entries.)

Arnold, Catharine, *City of Sin: London and its Vices*, Simon & Schuster, 2010.

Belloc, Hilaire, *The Four Men – a Farrago*, Thomas Nelson & Sons, 1912 and 1948. (Also www.homesteadbb.free-online.co.uk/sussex.html)

Bourne, Jo (Editor), *The Most Amazing Places of Folklore & Legend in Britain*, Reader's Digest, 2011. (Reference for several entries.)

Brandwood, Geoff, *Britain's Best Real Heritage Pubs*, St Albans, CAMRA, 2013 and 2016. (Reference for several entries.) (Editor) *Real Heritage Pubs of the North West*, St Albans, CAMRA, 2017.

Brown, Pete, *Shakespeare's Local*, Macmillan, 2012. (George Inn, Southwark.)

Bruning, Ted, *Historic Pubs of London*, Prion Books, 1998. (Reference for several entries, e.g. Dirty Dicks, Grapes, Prospect of Whitby.) (with Paulin, Keith) *David & Charles Book of Historic English Inns*, Newton Abbott, David & Charles, 1982. (Reference for several entries.)

Churchley, Richard, *Having a Drink Around Bidford*, Astwood, Astwood Publications, 2014. (Bidford-on-Avon entry. Also 'Bidford-on-Avon labelled by Shakespeare as a drinking town,' *Birmingham Post*, 30 May, 2013.)

Cooke, Anthony, *A History of Drinking: The Scottish Pub since 1700*, Edinburgh University Press, 2015.

Croot, Viv, *Salacious Sussex*, Alfriston, Snake River Press, 2009.

Dedman and Betteridge, *Godalming: Growth of a Town 5*, Godalming, County Branch Library, 1969.

Dobrzynski, Jan, *Shropshire's Historic Pubs*, Stroud, History Press, 2009. (with Turner, Keith) *Worcestershire's Historic Pubs*, Stroud, History Press, 2007.

East Grinstead Museum, *Rebuilding Bodies & Souls: The Story of the Guinea Pig Club*, West Sussex, East Grinstead Museum, 2018.

Fiber, Sally, *The Fitzroy, the Autobiography of a London Tavern*, Lewes, The Book Guild, 1995. (Fitzroy Tavern. Also 'London pub's Victorian makeover', the *Guardian*, 20 March 2018.)

Greenwood, Stuart, *Cragg Coiners Walk*, Hebden Bridge, Sephton Enterprise Publications, 1998. (Mytholmroyd entry.)

Groombridge, Garth, *Southampton in 50 Buildings*, Stroud, Amberley, 2016. (Southampton Dancing Man entry.)

Gwilliam, H.W., *Old Worcester People & Places (Vol. I)*, Worcester, Rose Hill House Teachers Centre, 1977. (Grimley entry.)

Hiscock, Robert, *A History of Gravesend*, Phillimore, 1985. (Gravesend entry.)

Holland, Richard, *Supernatural Clwyd, The Folk Tales of NE Wales*, Llanrwst, Gwas Carreg Gwalch, 1989. (Marford entry.)

Hopkinson, Frank, *The Joy of Pubs*, Portico Books, 2013.

Hornsey, Ian Spencer, *A History of Beer and Brewing*, Royal Society of Chemistry, 2003. (Leatherhead entry.)

Hurley, Heather, *Pubs of Monmouth, Chepstow and the Wye Valley*, Logaston Press, 2007. (Penallt entry.)

Ivers, Cliff, *Ye Olde Boar's Head: A Historical Guide to England's Oldest Public House*, Middleton Archaeological Society, 2017.

Jack, Albert, *The Old Dog & Duck: The Secret Meaning of Pub Names*, Penguin, 2011.

Jackson, Lee, *Palaces of Pleasure*, Yale University Press, 2019. (Highbury Barn and Eagle, Islington entries.)

Jones, Richard, *Myths & Legends of Britain & Ireland*, New Holland, 2003. *Haunted Inns of Britain & Ireland*, New Holland, 2004. (Tetbury entry.)

Kirby, Darrel, *The Story of Gloucester's Pubs*, Stroud, History Press, 2010.

Kissack, Keith, *The River Severn*, Lavenham, T. Dalton, 1982. (Bewdley entry.)

Larrington, Carolyne, *The Land of the Green Man: A Journey through the Supernatural Landscapes of the British Isles*, I.B. Tauris, 2015.

Martin, Brian, *Tales from the Country Pub*, Newton Abbott, David & Charles, 2001. (Ashleworth, Kings Walden and Prior's Dean entries.)

Medley, Paul and Dougill, John, *Pubs of Oxford & Oxfordshire*, Oxford, Oxface Publications, 2009. (Oxford and Headington entries.)

Moody, Paul and Turner, Robin, *The Search for the Perfect Pub*, Orion Books, 2011.

Nicholls, Robert, *Curiosities of Greater Manchester*, Stroud, Sutton Publishing, 2010. (Old Wellington and Sinclair's Oyster Bar entries.)

Oates, Jonathan, *John Christie of Rillington Place - Biography of a Serial Killer*, Barnsley, Pen & Sword Books, 2012. (Ladbroke Grove entry. Also p.6, Appendix 4, ACV Nomination for KPH, Ladbroke Association, undated.)

Protz, Roger, *Historic Coaching Inns of the Great North Road*, St Albans, CAMRA, 2017. (Editor), *Good Beer Guide 2019*, St Albans, CAMRA, 2018.

Rose, David, *Guildford Pubs*, Stroud, Amberley Books, 2016.

Russell, Ronald, *Waterside Pubs – Pubs of the Inland Waterways*, Newton Abbott, David & Charles, 1974.

Tierney-Jones, Adrian, *CAMRA's Great British Pubs*, St Albans, CAMRA, 2011. (Black Boy, Winchester entry.)

Thompson, Laura, *The Last Landlady: An English Memoir*, Unbound, 2018.

Townsend, Terry, *East Sussex Smugglers' Pubs*, Wellington, Pixz Books, 2018. (East Dean, Hooe, Pevensey and Hastings entries.)

Winn, Christopher, *I Never Knew That About the River Thames*, Ebury Press, 2010. (Pangbourne entry.)

Wood, Emma and Didcock, Keith, *A Brit Different: A Guide to the Eccentric Events & Curious Contests of Britain*, Punk Publishing, 2010.

Yaxley, Philip, *Wymondham's Old Inns*, Wymondham Heritage Society, 2017.

## Websites

CAMRA's national online pub guide, www.whatpub.com, has been invaluable for finding out basic details in advance of research visits.

Useful information on traditional and unusual events, many of which take place in or around pubs: http://calendarcustoms.com

www.fdca.org.uk/Chevalier_Johnstone.html (Broughty Ferry entry.)

www.dymchurch.org/history/inns.htm

www.beatlesource.com by Chazz Avery (Liverpool entry).

www.british-history.ac.uk/survey-london/vols43-4/pp313-326 (London Docklands entry).

www.edp24.co.uk/norfolk-life-2-1786/norfolk-history (Adam and Eve and Lollards Pit, Norwich entries.)

www.norfolkpubs.co.uk/norwich (Lollards Pit, Norwich entry).

https://queensferry-at-war.weebly.com/queensferry-history/a-brief-history-of-the-hawes-inn (South Queensferry entry).

http://hoaxes.org/af_database/permalink/left_handed_bar_glasses (Nicky-Tams, Stirling entry.)

https://burnhamgreen.com/history/the-headless-horse (Welwyn Garden City entry.)

https://historicengland.org.uk/listing/the-list/list-entry/1390020 (Worcester entry.)

www.greyhoundmarbles.com (Crawley entry.)

NB: In many cases, information was also garnered from articles, newspaper clippings and other items and plaques displayed inside and outside the pubs.

# INDEX OF PLACES

*The Tower Bank Arms in Near Sawrey, Cumbria.*

*The Hand at Llanarmon DC.*